STUDYING CURRICULUM

Studying Curriculum
Cases and Methods

IVOR F. GOODSON

Teachers College, Columbia University
New York and London

To Lily Goodson, my Mum,
'one of the best', with love and thanks

Published in the United States by Teachers College Press, 1994
Published in Great Britain by Open University Press

Library of Congress Cataloging-in-Publication Data

Goodson, Ivor.
  Studying curriculum : cases and methods / Ivor F. Goodson.
    p. cm.
  Includes bibliographical references and indexes.
  ISBN 0-8077-3362-8
  1. Education—Curricula—Philosophy.   2. Education—Curricula—
Case studies.   3. Education—Curricula—Research.   4. Curriculum
planning.   5. Curriculum change.   I. Title.
LB1570.G665   1994
375'.001—dc20   93-46385
                                                                      CIP

Printed in Great Britain

Contents

Acknowledgements

First of all, I would like to thank my family for all their help and support over many years: my Mum Lily and my late Dad Fred, Auntie Vic and Uncle Clay, cousins Victor and Judy, Neil, Mic, Dessie, Dave, Rodg, Will, Pib, Della and Judy; most precious of all, my wife Mary and son Andy.

Malcolm Clarkson has been an enduring source of support and pleasure over the past decade. Above all, I cherish his peculiarly British possession – a sharp and delightfully venomous sense of humour. Priceless!

Since arriving in Canada, I owe many friends a debt of gratitude; in particular, Dennis Thiessen, Bob Morgan and Pete Medway, three of my best and most treasured friends. At the University of Western Ontario, among many, I am particularly grateful to Allan Pitman, Sharon Haggerty, Sharon Rich, Jim Sanders, John McPeck, Rebecca Coulter, Anton Allahar, Jim Coté, Sam Clarke and Martin Kreiswirth, and to Odilla Van Delinder for her key role in the preparation of this manuscript. At the University of Rochester, my thanks go to Philip Wexler, Dale Dannefer, David Hursh, Warren Critchlow and Janet Wolf. A good deal of this book was written when I was an International Visiting Scholar at Stanford University in 1991. John Meyer, in Sociology, was a warm and hospitable host and I hugely enjoyed our discussions whilst walking in the California Redwoods; David Tyack was generous enough spontaneously to offer his office for my use and this made my stay even more enjoyable.

My co-workers on the SSHRC research projects, Ian Dowbiggin and Chris Anstead, have been a wonderful source of dialogue and debate; my thanks go to them as co-authors of Chapters 3, 4, 5 and 6. Gary McCulloch and Dennis Thiessen both read the manuscript in full and provided many helpful comments. Dennis Lawton and Stephen J. Ball offered valuable insights into particular chapters.

Finally, thanks go to Andy Hargreaves. He has patiently nagged at me to finish this book and I greatly value our ongoing conversations about work and life!

'Curriculum reform and curriculum theory' first appeared in the *Cambridge Journal of Education*, July 1989, pp. 131–41.

'On understanding curriculum: the alienation of curriculum theory' develops from a paper 'The alienation of curriculum theory' first published in *Curriculum Perspectives*, October 1987, and written from a Joint Symposium given with Elliot Eisner at the Institute of Educational Research, University of Oslo.

'Curriculum history, professionalization and the social construction of knowledge' appeared in *Curriculum and Teaching*, Summer 1990. Thanks to Falmer Press for permission to print.

'Vocational education and school reform' appeared in the *History of Education Review*, Volume 20, No. 1, 1991.

'Subject status and curriculum change: commercial education in London, Ontario, 1920–1940' appeared in *Paedagogica Historica*, Volume 29, No. 2, 1993.

' "Nations at risk" and "national curriculum" ' appeared in the *Journal of Education Policy*, and *The Politics of Education Association Yearbook*, 1990, pp. 219–232. Thanks to Falmer Press for permission to print.

'Studying curriculum: towards a social constructionist perspective' was the keynote lecture at the Fifth Nordic Association of Educational Research Congress in the University of Uppsala, March 1989. It was published in the *Journal of Curriculum Studies*, July/August 1990, pp. 299–312.

Our thanks to the Social Science and Humanities Research Council for Grant 410-89-0232 'Origins and destinations: curriculum and change at an Ontario, vocational high school 1900–1940', and for Grant 410-91-1975 'Racial/ethnocultural minority teachers: identities and careers'; to the Ministry of Education for Grant EO43 on 'Curriculum and context'; to the Ministry of Colleges and Universities for a Teacher Development Grant to study 'Teacher orientation'.

Critical Introduction

ANDY HARGREAVES

I know only too well that the honour of being asked to write a critical introduction to the work of one of our best contemporary educational thinkers is all too quickly overtaken by the burdensome obligation of having to produce it within the pressing timeframes of publication deadlines. Writing the critical introduction to Ivor Goodson's book is just such an honour, and also inescapably a burden. But it is a burden that carries with it great pleasures: of friendship, colleagueship and intellectual engagement.

Over more than a decade, Ivor Goodson and I have become both close colleagues and good friends. This framework of friendship and colleagueship has been both the medium and the outcome of remarkably similar backgrounds, interests and pursuits: common interests in the field of curriculum and teaching; a shared quest to make rational sense of a profoundly irrational social world; uncannily similar life and career trajectories; and, not least, closely matched intellectual styles that do not easily wince at criticism, in jest or in earnest, either in the giving or in the receipt.

Although it is somewhat unfashionable to declare it in the pluralistic, postmodern age, the distinctive trajectory that locates and delineates Ivor Goodson's work (and mine) is that of the English working-class boy proverbially 'made good'. To understand this life-course is to understand the nature of curriculum as an alien experience for Goodson the working-class student; to understand the drive to reclaim and reconstruct a sense of curriculum worthy of *all* students, for Goodson the adult; and to understand the grounded suspicion of hierarchies and orthodoxies within the school curriculum and within the intellectual study of it, for Goodson the scholar.

The biography of the upwardly mobile working-class male merits no special celebration; nor, within postmodern frameworks of multiple inequities (of gender, race, ethnicity, disability, etc.), does it call for self-deprecating apology. The trajectory and what follows from it, simply needs to be acknowledged for what it is. Were Goodson's trajectory that of a southern US black or a middle-class woman, for instance, quite different intellectual preferences and social perceptions would no doubt follow from it. But these are not Goodson's trajectories. While it is possible to connect intellectually and practically with the problems and concerns that spring from these other life patterns – and Goodson's book makes clear strides in doing so (especially in his analysis of the history of commercial education) – the matters closest to our hearts, our organizing frameworks of thought and action, inevitably spring from our own trajectories and the lives and experiences grounded within them.

To understand the work, you have to understand the life. This is no less true for professors of education than it is for the teachers they profess to study. The intellectual consequences of Goodson's own life course are most vividly present in two domains: in his substantive concern with the relationship between class, context and curriculum; and in the vigorously eclectic and at times proudly iconoclastic stance he adopts in relation to these things. It is these two aspects of Goodson's scholarship I want to examine and expand upon in some detail within this critical introduction, for it is here, I believe, that the distinctive contribution of his scholarship is to be found.

Class, context and curriculum

Since the 1960s, 'curriculum' has emerged as one of the most substantial fields of study within educational research and development. In his review for the US Association for Supervision, Curriculum and Development, of challenges and achievements in curriculum reform, William Schubert points to the 1970s, or specifically 1973–83, as a particularly prolific period of growth within curriculum studies, symbolized by the addition of the *Journal of Curriculum Theorizing, Journal of Curriculum and Supervision* and *Curriculum Perspectives* to the journals *Curriculum Inquiry* and the *Journal of Curriculum Studies* first established in 1968.[1]

Although the origins of curriculum theory, curriculum development and self-conscious curriculum practice extend much further back than the 1960s, to the foundational frameworks of Tyler and Taba, the optimistic and expansionist era commencing in the late 1960s was when the curriculum field flourished and redefined the core concerns of its field. These concerns expanded beyond the early behavioural frameworks of curriculum *aims and objectives*, to organizational processes of curriculum project *research and development* (Havelock, Shipman, Decker Walker), ensuing problems of curriculum *implementation* (Berman and McLaughlin, Gross and his colleagues), ubiquitous frameworks of *human meaning* through which people experienced and interpreted the curriculum (Pinar, Grumet, Greene) and profoundly practical processes of decision-making and *deliberation*, which defined curriculum not through reference to universal schemes and principles, but according to particular judgements of situation and circumstance (Schwab, Westbury, Reid).

Development (and implementation), *deliberation* and *decision-making* were the core concerns of the curriculum field at this time; the major preoccupations of the paradigm. Fundamental matters of curriculum definition, however, of who constructed the curriculum, within what kinds of political or epistemological parameters and for whose benefit, were largely neglected. A group of British analytic philosophers did dedicate themselves to defining philosophically the forms and fields of knowledge on which school curricula should be based (Hirst, Wilson, Phenix), but their concerns were marginal to mainstream curriculum discourse (although they would come into their own later when the drive to develop national and other centralized curricula sent people scurrying in search of prescriptive philosophical foundations).

As Goodson discerns in Chapter 1, 'the most important scholarship on curriculum . . . took place [during] . . . a period of unusual change and flux elsewhere in the Western world.' At this time, 'a wide range of curriculum reform movements were actively seeking to . . . revolutionize school curricula.' 'It was unlikely,' he continues, 'that scholars or curriculum reformers would wish to focus upon, let alone concede, the areas of stability, of unchallengeable "high ground" that may have existed within the school curriculum."' Implementation and interpretation were highlighted; definition and delineation were not. Goodson describes curriculum reform during this period as 'a sort of tidal wave [that] . . . created turbulence and activity but actually . . . only engulfed a few small islands.' The high ground, he says, was left completely untouched. This high ground is the written curriculum, how it is constructed and sustained, who are its guardians and who its beneficiaries. In the heyday of curriculum development and theorizing, for the reasons Goodson outlines, this high ground was untouched by most curriculum reform and unaddressed by the main body of curriculum theory.

What appear to be and are sometimes presented as the generic, constitutive concerns of contemporary curriculum theorizing – practical, deliberative, interpretive and humanistic – are therefore in most respects the particular preoccupations of a specific and arguably aberrant historical moment: one characterized by optimism and expansion in the political sphere, and relative autonomy and discretion in the professional one. The irony of all this is that now, when the practice of curriculum reform has rarely been more profoundly social, systemic and political in nature (in the pervasive preoccupations with national curricula, subject knowledge and the like), most of the curriculum field remains anachronistically anchored to issues of interpretation and implementation.

For instance, indigeneous English commentators on the National Curriculum of England and Wales have tended to emphasize the state's incapacity to implement the National Curriculum in practice. They point to institutional contingencies and departmental differences that produce variations in interpretation and implementation.[2] While these observed variations certainly ring true, and while curriculum policy clearly does not have a one-to-one correspondence with curriculum practice (even when such policy is imposed in great detail and with relentless political determination), my real concern (as Goodson's) is that scholarly and policy debate gets deflected from the fundamentals of curriculum definition and who controls it, to the complicated details of curriculum implementation. This is like looking at varied flight paths of locusts within a giant pestilential swarm rather than being concerned with the overall movement of the swarm itself and the livelihoods that are threatened by it. The political and practical significance of this deflection is highlighted, most perversely perhaps, by a post-Cold War, Russian Intourist guide quoted by John Pilger in his book *Distant Voices*. She describes how the old Soviet education system is being decentralized. When informed by British tourists about the development of the English National Curriculum, the guide retorts with exasperation (and more than a touch of relevant experience): 'A national curriculum? That's how you order minds not educate them. Are you objecting to this?'[3]

Not just in Britain, but in many other parts of the world, centralized written curricula are now being erected and imposed in ways that are reinventing traditional subjects and reasserting their value, often to the detriment of students who would benefit from educational experiences of a more relevant, flexible and culturally sensitive nature. Rarely have the fundamentals of curriculum construction been so palpably political in nature. Yet the bulk of the curriculum field remains narrowly preoccupied with the vagaries and vicissitudes of implementation, or with stories and narratives of personal curriculum meaning among introspective teachers in individual classrooms. In these most turbulent political times and precarious educational ones, curriculum theory seems seriously to be losing its way.

This is most disconcertingly the case, perhaps, in the one visibly emergent theoretical addition to the curriculum field: that which comprises poststructuralism and postmodernism. With their emphasis on the multiplicity of personal meanings that can be assigned to or derived from any particular curriculum text, and on the process of deconstructing educational or policy texts – to unearth these different possible meanings – poststructuralist and postmodernist approaches to curriculum theory betray a rather tragic retreat of the academy into the cloistered enclaves of esoteric intellectualism just when an articulate and accessible confrontation with the foundational assumptions of curriculum politics has scarcely been more needed. As I have recently argued elsewhere, 'the preoccupation with the personal, and the relative neglect of the social and political is a chronic feature of our postmodern social condition', where theoretical narcissism and therapeutic self-indulgence have become all too prevalent within curriculum theorizing.[4]

It is here, amid an intellectual field turning predominantly inward towards the institution and the individual, that the importance of Goodson's contribution to curriculum theory and research stands out. Goodson proposes, outlines and instantiates what he calls a *social constructionist* perspective to the study of curriculum. He plants this firmly in a 'middle ground' of subject traditions, departments and politics. This middle ground is a starting point from which to delve intimately into the lives and biographies of individuals who experience those traditions on the one hand; and to reach outwards to the antecedent structures which establish the assumptions underlying curriculum traditions on the other. This deceptively simple yet politically potent historical and social perspective is at the heart of Goodson's work and is amply illustrated with conceptual arguments and detailed empirical evidence throughout his book.

Here and elsewhere Goodson's work builds self-consciously and respectfully on the intellectual inheritance of a group of European scholars known as the 'new sociologists of education', who in the early 1970s applied very broad perspectives in the sociology of knowledge to the study of the school curriculum. The fundamental problem with which this group grappled was crystallized in Basil Bernstein's celebrated quotation that 'How a society selects, classifies, distributes, transmits and evaluates the educational knowledge it considers to be public reflects both the distribution of power and the principles of social control.'[5] These scholars were among the first to draw important and insightful distinctions between high-status knowledge and low-status knowledge: high-status knowledge is abstract, unrelated to everyday experience, easily assessed and largely written down; low-status knowledge is concrete, closely connected to out-of-school knowledge, harder to assess and more oral or practical in nature. What counted as valid knowledge, it was argued, was defined differently for and made selectively available to different groups.[6] For the first time, educational selection and inequality was seen to be not just an issue of resources or access or segregation into different schools or streams. It was also a question of curriculum: of the knowledge to which you had access; of who defined it and controlled it; and of how it did or did not relate to your own understanding and experience.

Curriculum here became clearly tied to social class. Much of the mainstream curriculum, it transpired, was alien to working-class interests and experience, in both its academic content and its didactic, subject-based form. Following this early theoretical promise, though, it was not into class that ensuing empirical work went, but into the classroom. As Goodson describes in Chapter 2, empirical researchers following the lead of the new sociology of education embarked upon studies of classroom interaction or undertook qualitative case studies of curriculum implementation. Although the new sociology of education raised questions about *both* the construction of curriculum *and* its realization through the details of interaction in the classroom, it was to the latter that empirical energies were subsequently directed. Important as classroom studies were, an opportunity to study the foundations and formation of the contemporary curriculum and its appropriateness for different groups was for the most part temporarily lost.

In the 1970s and early 1980s there were macro-theories of educational inequality and micro-theories of classroom interaction, but few ways to trace and explain the connections between the two. With a small number of other research studies (most notably Whitty's analysis of social studies teaching, and Ball and Lacey's investigation of English departments[7]), Goodson has used curriculum to create a much needed bridge between the two. Through his extensive studies of subject communities, traditions and identities, he has, more than anyone, built a deep understanding of how subjects are made, how they are sources of status and identity for teachers, what processes or 'evolutionary profiles' subject communities follow to raise their status over time, how school subjects are objects of political bargaining and conflict and how the pursuance of increased status for many subjects is antithetical to the interests of the most needy students who are exposed to them.

These are the realities of curriculum policy and practice. Teachers know them all too well – especially in secondary schools. They talk about them often – but through gossip and innuendo, in jokes and in gripes, in the staffroom and the parking lot. The raw realities of curriculum rarely form part of the official business of schooling, still less of curriculum policy review. Always there, they are rarely talked about openly. Academically and politically, too many curriculum realities have been kept 'off the table'. Instead, as Goodson indicates in Chapter 2, curriculum theory and policy have been dominated by the ideals of philosophical and psychological prescription, abstracted from the institutional realities of curriculum practice. Curriculum categories and curriculum policies have been based on philosophically speculative and speciously conservative 'forms of knowledge' that turn out to be uncannily like the traditional subjects from which social elites and their offspring have benefited for decades (this is often called having 'stood the test of time'). Or curriculum contents or processes are based on idealized psychological models of children's learning – be they Piagetian, Vygotskyian or constructivist – that try to address how children actually learn, but in doing so also ignore the real context of teaching, testing and resources in which that learning is located.

Goodson has achieved more than anyone in placing the realities of curriculum, in particular the history and politics of school subjects around which most curriculum is structured, 'on the table'. He has given curriculum a context. Nor has he done this just with elegant armchair theorizing (or even inelegant armchair theorizing – for there is much of that in the curriculum field too!). Particularly in the United States, a rich theoretical tradition of radical curriculum critique has grown up in the past two decades: pointing to the ideological underpinnings of curriculum, illustrating how much curriculum sustains dominant interests and helps reproduce the social structures from which dominant groups benefit; exposing the gaps and silences within existing curriculum discourse and the radical questions and concerns that are placed off teachers' and students' agendas because of this; and theorizing the strategies and alliances that are required to construct radical curriculum reforms of a more just and democratic nature. But while his work has been critical and challenging, it has also been developed largely in the absence of engagement with the concrete complexities of detailed empirical evidence. One thing I have consistently admired about Goodson's work, by contrast, is that it does not shrink from practical engagement with these historical and institutional complexities. In a manner that befits and is consistent with his own humble beginnings, Ivor Goodson is never afraid to get his hands dirty. Though always critical and creative in his theoretical approach, he also grapples extensively with the evidence, with all its uncomfortable uncertainties and complexities (there are perhaps rather too many other curriculum scholars – philosophical and otherwise – whose theorizing does not seem to be unduly cluttered or hampered by abundances of evidence).

Elsewhere, Ivor Goodson has undertaken meticulous histories of geography, biology, rural studies, European studies, computer education and other school subjects. In Chapters 5 and 6 of this book, he turns the hand of his empirical labours to vocational education and commercial education. That this is more than a kind of curricular train-spotting, ticking subject items off from the historical list, is clearly evidenced in Chapter 7, where Goodson uses his collected knowledge of subject and curriculum history to construct a quite devastating critique of the National Curriculum of England and Wales.

With cruel and telling irony, Goodson exposes the parallels between the subject-based National Curriculum of 1988, along with the categories that comprise it, and the subject-based Secondary Regulations of 1904. Showing his clear concern for the connection between curriculum and social class, Goodson sees in both sets of regulations a process of 'curriculum as social prioritizing'. The Secondary Regulations of 1904 defined the secondary school curriculum in such a way as to exclude technical and commercial subjects at which working-class students were disconcertingly beginning to display signs of success. The National Curriculum of 1988, with its excision of integrated studies, social studies, environmental education, political education, global education and even business studies as 'foundational' subjects, has similar consequences.

The contents and categories of curriculum are a powerful device of social selection and social control: in terms of gender and race, certainly, and in terms of social class as well. It is through this latter criterion that the contemporary curriculum secures its most invisible and arguably insidious divisions. Many employers now designate themselves as Equal Opportunities employers that do not discriminate according to gender, race, sexual orientation or disability. None, to my knowledge, proclaim that they do not discriminate according to social class. Yet it is through the content and categories of a curriculum that remains alien to much working-class experience that the achievements of working-class students which qualify them for or disqualify them from better employment and opportunities for social influence are fundamentally delimited and defined. In his analysis of the National Curriculum, Goodson clearly illustrates how class and context are in these ways absolutely central to the analysis of curriculum and the issues of who benefits from it.

The policy implications of Goodson's insights in particular and the history and politics of the school curriculum in general, as evidenced in the scholarship of writers like Barry Franklin, Herbert Kliebard, George Tomkins and David Layton, are immense. I have often pressured Ivor Goodson to take more of a public stand in pushing such policy implications further. My own research and analysis of secondary school curriculum reform for the Ministry of Education of Ontario, for instance, has been profoundly influenced by Goodson's work on the history, politics and social organization of school subjects. As a result, every secondary school in the province of Ontario now possesses a report, *Rights of Passage*, which talks about these issues of curriculum history, politics and social organization as profoundly practical problems – not as barriers to implementation, but as central subjects for redefinition and reform themselves.[8] The provincial curriculum reform agenda in Ontario now explicitly addresses issues of subject status and curriculum integration: of rigour and relevance for all students, not rigour for some and relevance for the rest; of a common curriculum that does not force status-based choices between different social groups, and so on. Goodson's work is political, yet it is also deeply practical (perhaps precisely because of that political realism). It provides a theoretically informed and empirically based 'middle ground' for the intellectual study of curriculum, and a politically realistic edge to its development. This, I believe, is his most significant contribution.

Meaning and marginality

Mobility brings with it marginality. As writers on marginality or 'liminality' have noted, those who are at the edge of their social group, who are transients or travellers, moving on the boundaries of social and intellectual life, are often the most critical and perceptive about the group's principles and problems.[9] Marginal men and women do not become rutted within the well-ploughed furrows of thought that order (and enclose) the social and intellectual self-understandings of the group. They do not succumb easily to group pressure, nor fall prey to fashionable paradigms of thought.

In marginality are to be found some of the most powerful sources of insight and creativity in social and intellectual life. In academic life, marginal men and women stand at the borders of intellectual fields and traditions: not to protect and patrol, but to extend and explore. Admired for their creativity on some occasions, ostracized for their non-conformity on others, marginal men and women peer critically but not dismissively into the assumptions and traditions of different fields, and make creative connections and contributions that often elude their colleagues who are too firmly rooted to particular traditions themselves. Steven Hawking's monumentally creative contribution to physical science, for instance, comes not from work *within* relativity theory nor from work *within* the field of quantum mechanics, but from work that connects and transcends the two.[10] Similarly, the celebrated Canadian geologist J. Tuzo Wilson, whose 'brilliant theory' of continental drift 'provided a unifying model for all of the large scale dynamics evident at the earth's surface', confessed before his death to having 'always been rather eclectic in my interests'.[11] Within the competing subfields of educational and curriculum research (which behave in ways not altogether unlike the competing subject communities of schooling), eclecticism is often a thinly veiled term of abuse, implying inferior scholarship or lack of rigour (at the same time, of course, such abuse also defends the purity of particular paradigms and those who prosper from them). Articles submitted to scholarly journals may be returned to their authors with referees' 'requests' that they locate their work within a particular tradition (I speak here from personal but by no means isolated experience!). In intellectual subfields just as in school subject communities, paradigms are purity and eclecticism is danger. At its best though, it is robust eclecticism of the kind that Goodson practises that makes creative connections across paradigms and does most to push the boundaries of our understanding further.

It is marginal men and women who take these risks. Theirs is often the distant voice, but also the most dissident one. They are the conscience of our intellectual culture. Goodson's creative contribution to curriculum theory stems from the distance and dissidence of the marginal man in three respects.

First, there are distinct elements of social marginality in Goodson's life and career trajectory. The son of a Berkshire labourer, Ivor Goodson may have moved into a world of professional privilege, but he draws extensively on the skills of enquiry and funds of knowledge that attach to this world to develop the craft of and pursue the commitment to social critique that is characteristic of his class of origin. Whatever his professional and social progress, Goodson's work is rooted in and continually returns to the concerns of his class. As a teacher at Countesthorpe College and Stantonbury Campus, two radical and innovative comprehensive schools of considerable renown and/or notoriety in the 1970s, Goodson strove to make curricula for and with working-class students – curricula that were not alien to their interests and experiences. In practical ways, he also sought to challenge the institutionalized regularities of schooling in the form of subjects, class teaching and the like, to create a curriculum, an education, that would be more meaningful and motivating for students who came from backgrounds like his.

Goodson's scholarship continues to express this return to his roots. His analyses of commercial education, vocational education and the National Curriculum are all analyses of curriculum as a process of class exclusion: exclusion from opportunity, exclusion from mobility and exclusion from rigorous, collective critique. The classifications of curriculum are shown to be closely tied to the class divisions of society. Goodson enunciates other concerns as well, of course – about gender equity in his discussion of commercial education, and about constructs of national identity in his critique of the National Curriculum – but his return to his roots retains class as a central concern alongside these.

Second, marginality and its associated creativity can come from geographical as well as social mobility. Having lived and researched extensively in England, Ivor Goodson (like myself) is now a professor of education in Canada. Like Australia or New Zealand, Canada is, in a sense, on the geographical periphery of Anglophone academic life. But as is certainly true for Australian educational research, it is on the periphery where the most exciting and innovative scholarship is often to be found. People on the periphery often need to work harder and read more voraciously and globally to feel and be connected to their colleagues and their fields. As a result, they are often better connected intellectually than many of their colleagues in imperial strongholds such as the United States and Great Britain, where approaches to writing and research are often deeply ethnocentric and exclusive in nature. Indeed, on any given topic, the bibliographies of texts from the two countries are often totally mutually exclusive. Goodson's writings and research embrace a broad panoply of scholarship: English, mainland European, Australian and North American. This gives his work relevance and rootedness to a broad variety of contexts, and lends it the vital critical edge that often follows from thoughtful comparative study and analysis. Countries like Canada may now be refuges for intellectual émigrés and homeless minds in the way the United States was in the 1930s to 1950s, but just like the United States in that period, they also often become centres of great intellectual originality that come from critical minds working in less repressive political contexts than the ones they left.

Third, in addition to social and geographical marginality, Ivor Goodson's work possesses elements of intellectual marginality. It straddles and transcends disciplinary boundaries. Goodson is a historian and a sociologist, a curriculum theorist and a researcher of teacher development – and he is accomplished in all these domains. Working across these boundaries is itself a spur to originality. But it is the historical orientation that is perhaps the most definitive. This historical orientation embraces both a scholarly quest and a personal one, which a metaphor will help me elucidate.

In a fictionalized account of the Australian Aboriginal 'dreamtime' or 'song-lines', Bruce Chatwin describes the role of song in Aboriginal myth and culture. As Chatwin records, Aboriginal 'songs' are more than oral records, myths or simple stories. Songs and singing have a central place in the Aboriginal understanding of human and natural creation. It was through song that the world was not just remembered and recorded, but created and recreated. 'By singing the world into existence . . . the Ancestors had been poets in the original sense of *poesis*, meaning "creation" . . . Aboriginals could not believe the country existed until they could see it and sing it – just as, in the Dream-time, the country had not existed until the Ancestors sang it.'[12]

Goodson's sense and use of history is rather like this. For Goodson, curriculum history records, returns to and reinstates the past, within the context of the present. It also recreates the present within the remembrance of the past: his work continually 'sings' the past and present into existence. In the ephemeral preoccupation with immediate curriculum issues that characterizes a lot of contemporary curriculum analysis, the fact that curriculum policy-makers are often singing their same old songs is often overlooked. By contrast, Goodson's 'songs' point to how contemporary issues are grounded in deep historical contexts. He points to the historical recurrence of status struggles surrounding vocational education, and of gender struggles surrounding commercial education – struggles that recur across decades. By singing these songs, Goodson awakens the past in the present, and helps us see the past again and anew. Here is the power of his study of institutional history and individual biographies: of a social constructionist perspective on curriculum that is historically grounded, contextually sensitive and empirically rich.

Conclusion

It is fashionable to point to our society as a pluralistic, postmodern one where decision-making is decentralized, influence is pluralistic, meaning is uncertain and voices are more diverse. While there is a lot of truth in these claims – indeed I have analysed the impact of the postmodern social condition on education extensively elsewhere[13] – the focus on complexity and diversity sometimes disguises and deflects attention from those areas of social life that have become considerably more centralized, more controlled and less negotiable than they were before. Curriculum, its centralization and politicization, is one of these. As Aronowitz and Giroux argue:

we need to preserve a notion of totality that privileges forms of analysis in which it is possible to make visible those mediations, interrelations and interdependencies that give shape and power to larger political and social systems. We need theories that express and articulate difference, but we also need to understand how the relations in which differences are constituted operate as part of a wider set of social, political and cultural practices.[14]

Anachronistically rooted in the expansionist era of the 1960s and its accompanying concerns with meaning, implementation and innovation, or inclined towards postmodernist poseurism and its preoccupations with differentiation and deconstruction, much contemporary curriculum theory is ill-equipped to engage with and critique the absolutely fundamental ways in which the written curriculum is being politically and socially redefined. Goodson's social constructionist perspective offers a fruitful approach for investigating the inescapable political realities of the contemporary curriculum; for analysing how the hegemonic boundaries of learning and thought are being reinstated or redrawn. Moreover, his adopted methods of history and biography should insure any followers or fellow travellers against the intellectual conceits that can sometimes ensue if imaginative theorizing is untempered by the constraints of evidence and the ordinary (and not just selectively appropriated) voices contained within it. This book is a highly promising starting point for a radical yet realistic perspective on curriculum in the current age. I believe that such a combination of conceptual and political radicalism and empirical and historical realism not only defines Goodson's scholarship but also demystifies the curriculum it addresses.

Introduction

This book comprises a set of studies that seek to link together the arguments for more historical, social constructionist study of the school curriculum. These studies have been written over a span of five years as part of an ongoing programme of work with a cohesive focus on the social construction of curriculum. The earlier chapters develop the arguments for such a methodological focus and later chapters provide some case studies of the social constructions that comprise curriculum prescription. In associated work, our research has gone on to explore the implications of preactive curriculum constructions for interactive process and practice.[1] Other work has focused on the implications for the teacher's life and work[2] and begun to explore the importance of this work at the level of text and discourse and to develop some genealogies of knowledge.[3] But in this book the focus is primarily on curriculum as socially onstructed prescription.

The reason for this sustained project is the continuing need to analyse and address the wide range of centralized and bureaucratic prescriptive curriculum that is now emerging. This rapid and accelerating movement needs to be closely monitored before we can understand the full range of implications for school processes, practices and discourses. Even though the focus in this book is on preactive prescription the scholarly project should move into studies of interactive realization and textual embodiment and interpretation. Social constructionist study of prescriptive curricula then forms one point of a counter-cultural axis which spans interpretive and naturalistic studies of practice and deconstructionist studies of discourse and text. Our understanding of each of these elements should complement and extend our understanding of the other.

In the first chapter, I begin to lay out the arguments for a more historical and contextualized focus on the social construction of preactive school curriculum. The change towards the National Curriculum in the United Kingdom is examined as an instance where such work should be undertaken (this theme is later picked up in Chapter 7). The National Curriculum in the UK has led to a wide range of initiatives and a continuing flurry of activity. As always, frenetic activity in the foreground tends to obscure some of the deeper continuities in the background. Hence, if I harp on about the need for historical context and complain about its absence, it is with some knowledge of how frenetic and turbulent matters have been in the world of state schooling in the UK. In such difficult times, a range of studies have begun to emerge which seek to locate the National Curriculum initiative,[4] and the studies in the book should be seen as part of that broader collective project, pursued in ways that seek to fill the gaps surrounding preactive curriculum construction.

In Chapter 2, the lacunae and omissions of curriculum theory over the past decades, particularly the 1960s and 1970s, are examined, critiqued and to some extent themselves located as historically embedded social constructions. The argument for focusing on the 'middle ground' of curriculum construction is presented together with some scrutiny of the dangers that go with a failure to develop historical perspectives. While the genealogy of curriculum studies presented is undoubtedly partial (it would be difficult for it to be any more in a brief section of one chapter), the purpose is to highlight the dangers implicit in belief in prescriptive givenness together with the associated dangers of a reaction that moves to transcend prescription altogether. Given the deconstructionist and poststructuralist impulse at the moment, it is possible to doubt that the contest over curriculum and the institutionalized categories that comprise curriculum sites of action is really important. For curriculum can indeed be reinterpreted, text can be deconstructed, every prescription can be subverted, inverted, converted or perverted. These are vital truths but the deconstructive impulse complements but does not contradict the impulse that studies the social construction of prescription. Such work does not contradict the scholarly impulse to study the processes of definition and delineation which are central to the preactive construction of curriculum and the social priorities embedded within that curriculum. Prescriptions do indeed set parameters for schooling and curriculum; here the definitions and delineations circumscribe what is 'cultural' or 'social', what is of status and significance. The dissident, it is true, can transcend but the conformist majority is more likely to bend. In Foucault's sense, schooling and curriculum do remain successful disciplinary devices, managing populations and subjectivities with considerable dexterity. The social construction of the preactive curriculum is a vital and still substantially unexplored element of these devices and desires.[5]

Even at the very level of the critique developed herein the force of subject politics is clear. Sociology of the curriculum has in Ahier's words been 'institutionally marginalized and lost'.[6] This result of the politics of subjects, the unsuccessful battle over the curriculum, itself substantially affects the discourses and disputes which now take place. The barrenness of the field then confirms the general point that is being made.

Chapters 3 and 4 move on to a more positive mode in arguing the case for grounded historical studies of education. In passing, the current state of historical studies of education is scrutinized and some reasons are advanced as to why such work has tended to remain outside the schoolhouse door. Again, much of the explanation for this would appear to turn on the genealogies of subjects and their modes of enquiry. It is most clearly time to push historical studies through the schoolhouse door and into a confrontation with how preactive curricula define and delineate the practices of schooling.

Chapter 4 introduces the study of the London (Ontario) Technical and Commercial High School. This study began within months of my move to North America in 1986 and has been, most fortunately, sustained by a series of grants from the Social Science and Humanities Research Council of Canada. This Research Council has shown unusual regard for historical work and, as a result, a wide range of studies have been funded that go some way to addressing 'curriculum amnesia' in this country. As noted earlier, the chain of potential conversion and subversion is long in the journey from original curriculum conception and prescription to individual subjective inscription. But a large part of this chain covers the preactive stage: prescriptions are conceived of and issued by central states and local bureaucracies. They then pass to sites of institutional prescription – guideline subjects syllabuses are mediated and reformed at the preactive level as they are institutionalized. They are likely once again to be mediated at preactive level by individual subject departments and subject teachers. The preactive level of curriculum definition is a major chain of negotiation and transformation and one that is substantially unexplored.

Understanding the process of social construction of knowledge at this stage is of increasing importance in current times. As Wexler has cogently argued, the crucial question for curriculum theorists is how to move beyond conceptions of reproduction and resistance to a grounded understanding of how knowledge is produced, particularly, he argues, how new knowledge is produced for a post-Fordist world.[7]

Chapters 5 and 6 examine particular aspects of our continuing work at the school. The work reviewed in Chapter 5 provides a broad analysis of the context of vocational reform as this impinged on the school under study. The prescriptions and guidelines provided at provincial and local level were quite general and undirective when viewed from the present. But such a Whiggish interpretation should not obscure the strong social forces promoting vocational education in the particular local milieux under study.

Chapter 6 deals with a particular episode in the curriculum history of the school relating to commercial education. The struggle over commercial education was interlinked with the patterns of gender and the origins and destinations of the school students. For a wider summary of work on the school, readers are directed towards our new study, *Through the Schoolhouse Door*.[8]

From immersion in the 'middle ground' of a particular school in a particular place during a particular period, Chapter 7 moves our gaze to wider national and global initiatives as they emanate in the phenomenon, emergent in a number of countries, of 'national curriculum'. Here the concerns first raised in Chapter 1 are revisited. This essay was written for the *American Politics of Education Yearbook*. I have closely considered attempting to bring it up to date in this book. However, so fluid (and indeed unstable) is the situation in Britain (as I write this introduction, there is a case before the High Court to judge if teachers can boycott the National Curriculum tests) that it is like providing snapshots of a fast-moving target. I have, in the end, decided as my family would say 'to leave well alone'. Readers are urged to consult the latest edicts emerging from the offices of the increasingly transient Secretaries of State for Education at Westminster for the latest details. The work of Graham and Tytler has now illuminated the political priorities and short-sighted opportunism – which in fact operated in the case of history within the National Curriculum. Gary McCulloch in a spirited inaugural lecture has inveighed against the retreat from civic values that is epitomized by these episodes. He sets this against the period of the 1944 Education Act: 'The settlement of 1944 emphasised the aspirations of education as a civic project. It is the disintegration of or retreat from this project that surely represents one of the key shifts since the 1940s, against which the reforms of the 1990s need to be understood.'9 The absence of a civic mission, of a sense of what society it wants to create, leaves a sense of disarray at the heart of the National Curriculum. McCulloch concludes: 'Unless the Government is able to address these issues, it seems most unlikely to establish a settlement that will last as long as did that of the 1940s. If it does not, it will surely continue the frantic paperchase of the past fifteen years until it subsides into exhaustion and disillusionment.'10

In the final chapter, Chapter 8, a summary programme for the kind of work being advocated is provided. As will be seen, work is emerging in many countries at an increasingly rapid pace. There is, certainly from where I sit, a sense of intellectual momentum to this field of study. Perhaps there is an element of wishful thinking in this final statement, for it is a matter of urgent concern that the new social constructions under way in the world of the school curriculum be provided with a detailed historical context and commentary. Such work will always remind us that what can be socially constructed can also be deconstructed and reconstructed, and in this way it might yet be possible to reconstitute and reinscribe notions of social equity and justice.

1 Curriculum Reform and Curriculum Theory: A Case of Historical Amnesia

The school curriculum is a social artifact, conceived of and made for deliberate human purposes. It is therefore a supreme paradox that in many accounts of schooling the written curriculum, this most manifest of social constructions, has been treated as a 'given'. Moreover, the problem has been compounded by the fact that it has often been treated as a neutral given embedded in an otherwise meaningful and complex situation. Yet in our own schooling we know very well that while we loved some subjects, topics or lessons, we hated others. Some we learnt easily and willingly, others we rejected wholeheartedly. Sometimes the variable was the teacher, or the time, or the room, or us, but often it was the form or content of the curriculum itself. Of course, beyond such individualistic responses there were, and are, significant collective responses to curriculum and when patterns can be discerned they suggest this is far from a 'neutral' factor.

Why then, has so little attention been given to the making of curriculum? We have a social construction which sits at the heart of the process by which we educate our children. Yet in spite of the patchy exhortations of sociologists, sociologists of knowledge in particular, one looks in vain for serious study of the process of social construction that emanates as curriculum. The reasons for this lacuna in our social and educational studies can be focused on two specific aspects: first, the nature of curriculum as a source for study; second, associated with this, questions relating to the methods we employ in approaching the study of curriculum.

In this chapter I shall deal with some of the problems involved in employing curriculum as a source. Part of the problem has already been mentioned: namely that many accounts of schooling accept the curriculum as a given, an inevitable and essentially unimportant variable. (Of course, some important work in the fields of curriculum studies and sociology of knowledge have provided a continuing challenge to this kind of curriculum myopia.) But once it is accepted that the curriculum itself is an important source for study a number of further problems surface, for 'the curriculum' is a perennially elusive and multifaceted concept. The curriculum is such a slippery concept because it is defined, redefined and negotiated at a number of levels and in a number of arenas. It would be impossible to arbitrate over which points in the ongoing negotiations were critical. In addition, the terrain differs substantially according to local or national structures and patterns. In such a shifting and unfocused terrain it is plainly problematic to try to define common ground for our study. After all, if there is a lacuna in our study it is likely to be for good reasons.

The substantial difficulties do not, however, mean, as has often been the case to date, that we should ignore the area of curriculum as social construction completely or focus on 'minute particulars' that are amenable to focused study. Part of the problem is, I believe, resolvable. This resolution turns on identifying common ground or, conceptualized another way, some areas of stability within the apparent fluidity and flux of curriculum.

We should remember that a great deal of the most important scholarship on curriculum, certainly on curriculum as a social construction, took place in the 1960s and early 1970s. This was, however, a period of considerable change and flux everywhere in the Western world; and nowhere more so than in the world of schooling in general and curriculum in particular. For such a burgeoning of critical curriculum scholarship to happen during such times was both encouraging and, in a sense, symptomatic. The emergence of a field of study of curriculum as social construction was an important new direction. But, while itself symptomatic of a period of social questioning and criticism this burgeoning of critical scholarship was not without its down-side.

I believe that down-side has two aspects which are important as we begin to reconstitute our study of schooling and curriculum. First, influential scholars in the field often took a value position which assumed that schooling should be reformed, root and branch – 'revolutionized', the 'maps of learning redrawn'. Second, this scholarship took place at a time when a wide range of curriculum reform movements (which themselves carried a cadre of scholarly advisers) were actively seeking to do precisely this, 'to revolutionize school curricula'. Therefore it was unlikely that scholars or curriculum reformers would wish to focus upon, let alone concede, the areas of stability, of unchallengeable 'high ground' that may have existed within the school curriculum.

One might characterize curriculum reform in the 1960s as a sort of 'tidal wave'. Everywhere the waves created turbulence and activity but actually they only engulfed a few small islands; more substantial land masses were hardly affected at all, and on dry land the mountains, the high ground, remained completely untouched. As the tide now rapidly recedes the high ground can be seen in stark silhouette. If nothing else, our scrutiny of the curriculum reform should allow recognition that there is not only high ground but common ground in the world of curriculum.

Standing out more clearly than ever on the new horizon is the school subject, the 'basic' or 'traditional' subject. Throughout the Western world there is exhortation of but also evidence about a 'return to basics', a reconstitution of 'traditional subjects'. In England and Wales, for instance, the 'new' National Curriculum defines a range of subjects to be taught as a 'core' curriculum in all schools. The subjects thereby reinstated bear an uncanny resemblance to the list which generally defined secondary school subjects in the 1904 Regulations. *The Times Educational Supplement* commented about this reassertion of traditional subject dominance: 'The first thing to say about this whole exercise is that it unwinds 80 years of English (and Welsh) educational history. It is a case of go back to Go.' In the early years of the twentieth century the first state secondary schools were organized. Their curriculum was presented by the national Board of Education under the detailed guidance of Sir Robert Morant:

> The course should provide for instruction in the English Language and Literature, at least one Language other than English, Geography, History, Mathematics, Science and Drawing, with due provision for Manual Work and Physical Exercises, and in a girls' school for Housewifery. Not less than 4½ hours per week must be allotted to English, Geography and History; not less than 3½ hours to the Language where one is taken or less than 6 hours where two are taken; and not less than 7½ hours to Science and Mathematics, of which at least 3 must be for Science.

But in looking at the new National Curriculum, we find that: 'The 8–10 Subject timetable which the discussion paper draws up has as academic a look to it as anything Sir Robert Morant could have dreamed up.'[1] Likewise, in scrutinizing an earlier curriculum history in the US high school, Kliebard has pointed to the saliency of the 'traditional' school subjects in the face of waves of curriculum reform initiatives from previous decades. He characterizes the school subject within the US high school curriculum at this time as 'the Impregnable Fortress'.[2]

Let us return to the conceptualization of curriculum as our source of study, for it remains elusive and slippery, even in these times of centrality and tradition where we return to basics. In the 1960s and 1970s critical studies of curriculum as social construction pointed to the school classroom as the site wherein the curriculum was negotiated and realized. The classroom was the 'centre of action', 'the arena of resistance'. By this view what went on in the classroom *was* the curriculum (for a more detailed account see Chapter 2). The definition of curriculum – the view from the high ground and the mountains – was, it was thought, not just subject to redefinition at classroom level but quite simply irrelevant. Interestingly, some recent British work on the National Curriculum continues this myopia, focusing on resistance and redefinition at school level while signally failing to analyse the ideological and political battles over curriculum at the state level.

Such a view, and such a standpoint from which to begin to study curriculum, is, I think, unsustainable (and I would argue further, from my own social location, morally and politically unconscionable). Certainly the high ground of the written curriculum is subject to renegotiation at lower levels, notably the classroom. But the view, common in the 1960s, that it is therefore irrelevant is much less common nowadays. Initiatives such as the National Curriculum should have demolished such commonly held complacencies. In the high ground what is to be 'basic' and 'traditional' is reconstituted and reinvented.

The 'given' status of school subject knowledge is therein reinvented and reasserted. But this is more than political manoeuvring or rhetoric: such reassertion affects the discourse about schooling and relates to the 'parameters of practice'. In the 1990s it would, I think, be folly to ignore the central importance of the redefinition of the written curriculum. The written curriculum is the visible and public testimony of selected rationales and legitimating rhetoric for schooling. I have argued elsewhere that in England and Wales the written curriculum

> both promulgates and underpins certain basic intentions of schooling as they are operationalized in structures and institutions. To take a common convention in preactive curriculum, the school subject: while the written curriculum defines the rationales and rhetoric of the subject, this is the only tangible aspect of a patterning of resources, finances and examinations and associated material and career interests. In this symbiosis, it is as though the written curriculum provides a guide to the legitimating rhetorics of schooling as they are promoted through patterns of resource allocation, status attribution and career distribution. In short, the written curriculum provides us with a testimony, a documentary source, a changing map of the terrain: it is also one of the best official guide books to the institutionalized structure of schooling.[3]

What is most important to stress is that the written curriculum, notably the convention of the school subject, has, in this instance, not only symbolic but also practical significance: symbolic in that certain intentions for schooling are thereby publicly signified and legitimated; practical in that these written conventions are rewarded with finance and resource allocation and with the associated work and career benefits.

Our study of the written curriculum should afford a range of insights into schooling. But it is important to stress that such study must be allied to other kinds of educational study – in particular studies of school process, of school texts, of school assessment and of the history of pedagogy. This must be grounded within an understanding of the general social and economic history of the times, as the current salience of 'markets', privatization and globalization indicates; for schooling is comprised of the interlinked matrix of these elements and, indeed, other vital ingredients. With regard to schooling and to curriculum in particular, the final question is 'Who gets what and what do they do with it?'

The definition of written curriculum is part of this story. And that is not the same as asserting a direct or easily discernible relationship between the preactive definition of written curriculum and its interactive realization in classrooms. It is, however, to assert that the written curriculum most often sets important parameters for classroom practice (not always, not at all times, not in all classrooms, but 'most often'). The study of written curriculum will, first, increase our understanding of the influences and interests active at the preactive level. Second, this understanding will further our knowledge of the values and purposes represented in schooling and the manner in which preactive definition, notwithstanding individual and local variations, may set parameters for interactive realization and negotiation in the classroom and school, as well as for discourse construction and textual production.

Studies of the preactive in relationship to the interactive are, then, where we should end. But for the moment so neglected is the study of the preactive definition of written curriculum that no such marriage of methodologies could be consummated. The first step is plainly to undertake a range of studies of the definitions of written curriculum and, in particular, to focus on the 'impregnable fortress' of the school subject.

Reconstituting school subjects: the example of England and Wales in the 1980s and early 1990s

Traditionally in England and Wales those stressing 'the basics' have referred to the 3 Rs – reading, writing and arithmetic. In the 1980s and early 1990s it would be fair to say that those with curriculum power were following a new version of the 3 Rs – rehabilitation, reinvention and reconstitution. Often the rehabilitation strategy for school subjects in the 1980s took the form of arguing that good teaching is in fact good subject teaching. This is to seek to draw a veil over the whole experience of the 1960s, to seek to forget that many curriculum reforms were developed to try to provide antidotes to the perceived failures and inadequacies of conventional subject teaching. The rehabilitation strategy is itself in this sense quintessentially ahistorical but paradoxically it is also a reminder of the power of 'vestiges of the past' to survive, revive and reproduce.

In England the 'reinvention' of 'traditional' subjects began in 1969 with the issue of the first collection of Black Papers.[4] The writers in this collection argued that teachers had been too greatly influenced by progressive theories of education, such as the integration of subjects, mixed ability teaching, enquiry and discovery teaching. This resulted in neglect of subject and basic skill teaching and led to reduced standards of pupil achievement and school discipline; the traditional subject was thereby equated with social and moral discipline. The rehabilitation of the traditional subject promised the re-establishment of discipline in both these ways. The Black Papers were taken up by politicians and in 1976 the Labour Prime Minister James Callaghan embraced many of their themes in his Ruskin Speech. Specific recommendations soon followed. In 1979, for instance, following a survey of secondary schools in England and Wales, Her Majesty's Inspectorate drew attention to what they judged to be evidence of insufficient match in many schools between the qualification and experience of teachers and the work they were undertaking;[5] later in a survey of middle schools they found that higher standards of work overall were associated with a greater degree of use of subject teachers.[6]

These assertions and perceptions provided a background to the Department of Education pamphlet *Teaching Quality*. The Secretary of State for Education listed the criteria for initial teacher training courses. The first criteria imposed a requirement that the higher education and initial training of all qualified teachers should include at least two full years' course time devoted to subject studies at a level appropriate to higher education. This requirement therefore 'would recognize teachers' needs for subject expertise if they are to have the confidence and ability to enthuse pupils and respond to their curiosity in their chosen subject fields.'[7]

This final sentence is curiously circular. Obviously if the pupils choose subjects then it is probable that teachers will require subject expertise. But this is to foreclose a whole debate about whether they should choose traditional subjects as an educational vehicle. Instead, we have a political *fait accompli* presented as a dispassionate educational choice. In fact the students have no choice except to embrace 'their chosen subject fields'. The political rehabilitation of subjects by political diktat is presented as pupil choice.

In *Teaching Quality*, the issue of the match between the teachers' qualifications and their work with pupils, first raised in the 1979 HMI document, is again employed. We learn that 'the Government attach high priority to improving the fit between teachers' qualifications and their tasks as one means of improving the quality of education.'[8] The criterion for such a fit is based on a clear belief in the sequential and hierarchical pattern of subject learning: 'All specialist subject teaching during the secondary phase requires teachers whose study of the subject concerned was at a level appropriate to higher education, represented a substantial part of the total higher education and training period and built on a suitable A level base.'[9]

The beginning of subject specialization is best evidenced where the issue of non-subject based work in schools is scrutinized. Many aspects of school work take place outside (or beside) subject work – studies of school process have indeed shown how integrated, pastoral and remedial work originates because pupils, for one reason or another, do *not* achieve in traditional subjects. Far from accepting the subject as an educational vehicle with severe limits if the intention is to educate all pupils, the document seeks to rehabilitate subjects even in those domains which often originate from subject 'fall-out'.

> Secondary teaching is not all subject based, and initial training and qualifications cannot provide an adequate preparation for the whole range of secondary school work. For example, teachers engaged in careers or remedial work or in providing group courses of vocational preparation, and those given the responsibility for meeting 'special needs' in ordinary schools, need to undertake these tasks not only on the basis of initial qualifications but after experience of teaching a specialist subject and preferably after appropriate post-experience training. Work of this kind and the teaching of interdisciplinary studies are normally best shared among teachers with varied and appropriate specialist qualifications and expertise.[10]

The rehabilitation of school subjects has become the mainstay of government thinking about the school curriculum. In many ways the governmental and structural support offered to school subjects as the organizing device for secondary schooling is reaching unprecedented levels. Hargreaves has judged that 'more than at any time previously, it seems, the subject is to take an overriding importance in the background preparation and curricular responsibility of secondary school teachers.' But the preferred policy sits alongside a major change in the style of governance of education, for Hargreaves argues that

> nor does that intention on the part of HMI and DES amount to just a dishing out of vague advice. Rather, in a style of centralized policy intervention and review with which we in Britain are becoming increasingly familiar in the 1980s, it is supported by strong and clear declarations of intent to build the achievement of subject match into the criteria for approval (or not) of teacher training courses, and to undertake five yearly reviews of selected secondary schools to ensure that subject match is being improved within them and is being reflected in the pattern of teacher appointments.[11]

The associated issue of increasingly centralized control is also raised in a DES publication on education from 8 to 12 in combined and middle schools.[12] Again, the rehabilitation of school subjects is rehearsed in a section on the need to 'extend teachers' subject knowledge'. Rowland has seen the document as 'part of an attempt to bring a degree of centralized control over education'. He states that 'Education 8 to 12 may well be interpreted by teachers and others as recommending yet another means in the trend towards a more schematicized approach to learning in which the focus is placed even more firmly on the subject matter rather than the child.' He adds cryptically that the evidence it provides actually 'points to the need to move in quite the opposite direction'.[13] His reservations about the effects of rehabilitating school subjects are shared by other critics. Hargreaves has noted that one effect of the strategy 'will be to reinforce the existing culture of secondary teaching and thereby inhibit curricular and pedagogic innovation on a school-wide front'.[14]

The various government initiatives and reports since 1976 have shown a consistent tendency to return to 'basics', to re-embrace 'traditional' subjects. This government project, which spans both Labour and Conservative administrations, has culminated in the 'new' National Curriculum. The curriculum was defined in a consultative document, *The National Curriculum 5–16*. This was rapidly followed in the wake of the Conservatives' third election victory by the passing of the Education Reform Act in the House of Commons in 1988. The Act defines the National Curriculum, certain common curricular elements which are to be offered to pupils of compulsory school age. While it is presented as a striking new political initiative, comparison with the 1904 Regulations shows the remarkable degree of historical resonance. The National Curriculum comprises: the 'core' subjects of mathematics, English and science; and the 'foundation' subjects of history, geography, technology, music, art, physical education and (for secondary pupils) a modern foreign language[15] (for further discussion see Chapter 8).

Developing historical perspectives

Following the frustrating results of curriculum reform efforts in the 1960s and their substantial dismantling and reversal in the 1980s and early 1990s, the arguments for historical study are now considerable indeed. The contemporary power of those 'vestiges of the past', traditional school subjects, has been evidenced with instances drawn from Great Britain. To argue for curricular change strategies that ignored history would surely be an improbable, if not impossible, route in the current situation. Yet as we shall see this has been the dominant posture of curricular activists and theorists in the twentieth century. It is time to place historical study at the centre of the curriculum enterprise, to exhume the early work on curricular history, and the spasmodic subsequent work, and systematically to rehabilitate the study of the social construction of school subjects and the school curriculum.

In this introductory first section, the written curriculum is identified as a major but neglected historical source with which to develop our investigations of schooling. It becomes clear that just as the search for new sources moves us into neglected territory so too the search for an associated modality of study will require methods seldom used or at least seldom integrated in the study of schooling. Methods are required which allow us to study curriculum as it impinges on individual experiences of schooling as well as the experiences and social activities of social groups. Exploring curriculum as social construction allows us to study, indeed exhorts us to study, the intersection of individual biography and social structure. The emergence of curriculum as a concept came from a concern to direct and control individual teachers' and pupils' classroom activities. The definition of curriculum developed over time as part of an institutionalized and structured pattern of state schooling. Our methods therefore have to cover the analysis of individual lives and biographies as well as of social groups, structures and forces.

For this reason we should employ a range of methods from life histories of individual teachers through to histories of school subjects where the interplay of groups and structures is scrutinized. Relationships between individual and collective, between action and structures, are perennially elusive. However, our studies may either accept or exacerbate fragmentation or seek integration. Life history study pursued alongside the study of more collective groupings and milieux might promote better integration. The difficulty of integration is partly a problem of dealing with modes and levels of consciousness. The life history helps penetrate the individual subject's consciousness and also attempts to map the changes in that consciousness over the life cycle. But at the individual level as at other levels we must note that change is structured, but that structures change. The relationship between the individual and wider structures is central to our investigations but again it is through historical studies that such investigations might be most profitably pursued: 'Our chance to understand how smaller milieux and larger structures interact, and our chance to understand the larger causes at work in these limited milieux, thus require us to deal with historical materials.'[16]

The problems of elucidating the symbiosis of the individual and the social structure can be seen in the assessment of the broad goals of curriculum or schooling. The discerning of 'regularities', 'recurrences' or patterns is particularly elusive at the level of the individual life (and consciousness). Walter

Feinberg has noted that 'once we understand that a goal is identified in terms of something that is reasonably distinctive and that establishes relevance by postulating a continuity to otherwise discrete acts then we can see that goals may belong to individuals, but they may also belong to individuals as they are related to each other in acts or institutions.' He provides an example of people in America moving westwards, 'colonizing the west', which they did for many reasons:

> Some went to escape debt, others to make a fortune; some went to farm, others to pan gold, or to sell merchandise; some went as soldiers, others as trappers and hunters. Whereas it is perfectly proper to speak about the continuity of any series of acts performed by an individual in terms of a goal it is equally appropriate to speak of a whole series of acts performed by different individuals along with the acts of the government that supported them, such as the Homestead Act and the building of railroads, in terms of the *general* goal of settling the west. It is this way of speaking that allows us to make sense of all these acts and to see them as forming some kind of continuous meaningful event.[17]

The dangers of 'abstraction' to the general level are evidential and can be seen when Feinberg adds: 'Moreover, it is equally appropriate to speak of the goal as beginning with the movement of the first settlers west, even though these people may not have had a whisper of an idea about the overall historical significance of their act.'

Understood in this manner, structural change provides a facilitating arena for a range of individual actions which then feed into and act upon this initial change. Consciousness of the significance of the action differs according to the time period in question and the level of scrutiny – hence a series of individual 'dreams' and actions build up into a movement to 'colonize' a vast territory. Likewise, with schooling and curriculum discerning regularities, recurrences and patterns allows analysis and assessment of goals and intentions. 'To begin to characterise these goals by looking back to the origins of the school system itself is not necessarily to claim that the goals were fully understood at the time. It is simply to say that in the light of these goals we can understand some of the major lines of continuity between the activity of the past and the activity of the present.'[18]

Development of our studies of curriculum at individual and collective level demands that our historical analyses work across the levels of individual lives and group action and assess relations between individuals, between groups and between individuals and groups. Such work is reminiscent of Esland's early exhortations to develop frameworks 'for the analysis of the knowledge which constitutes the life world of teachers and pupils in particular educational institutions, and the epistemological traditions in which they collectively participate'. The intentions are very similar: 'trying to focus the individual biography in its sociohistorical context is in a very real sense attempting to penetrate the symbolic drift of school knowledge, and the consequences for the individuals who are caught up in it and attempting to construct their reality through it.'[19]

Histories of the symbolic drift of school knowledge raise questions about the patterns of change through which subjects pass. There is a growing body of work on the history of school subjects. These studies reflect a growing interest in the history of curriculum and besides elucidating the symbolic drift of school knowledge raise central questions about past and current 'explanations' of school subjects, whether they be sociological or philosophical.

Above all, this work illustrates the historical background, emergence and construction of the political economy of curriculum. The structure of resources and finance and the attribution of status and careers are linked to a system that has developed since the foundation of state schooling. This structure impinges on both individual intentions and collective aspirations. By focusing our studies on the historical emergence and reconstruction of structures and the ongoing activities of individuals and groups we might progressively alleviate the current amnesia. The written curriculum would begin to emerge as a major battle-ground where the futures and lives of generations of school students are influenced in crucial, yet so far substantially mystified, ways.

2 On Understanding Curriculum: The Alienation of Curriculum Theory

The present relationship between curriculum and curriculum theory is one of profound alienation. I use the term alienation in its more traditional derivation from the adjective 'alien' which the *Concise Oxford Dictionary* defines as 'not one's own; foreign, under foreign allegiance; differing in character, repugnant'.[1]

Curriculum theory and curriculum study are closely interlinked since curriculum studies feed into theory but also, perhaps more importantly, because theoretical paradigms guide the general directions and aspirations of curriculum study. The reconceptualization, for which I shall later argue, will involve both the manner in which we study curriculum and also that in which we develop theory. By developing historical studies of the social construction of curriculum it will be contended that our theoretical focus, and therefore the general character of our studies, might be refined and redefined.

The value of curriculum theory must be judged against the existing curriculum as defined and as negotiated and realized in schools. But contemporary curriculum theories do not generally seek to explain or theorize about what is evidential, what is there. They are not theories of curriculum but merely programmes. They are utopian not realist, concerned only with what should or might be, not with the art of the possible. They act not to explain but to exhort.

This alienation of theory from reality means that we encounter fundamental problems in creating educational policy in the face of a predominance of curriculum theories as *prescriptions*, (or, in Reid's words, as 'idealized practice').[2] The link between theory and policy is seldom perfect or direct. Whilst perhaps over-optimistic, Wise has warned that

> No matter how educational policy is created, its purpose is to affect (presumably to improve) the practice of education. Inevitably it must be based upon some theories or hypotheses about educational practice. If these assumptions are correct the policy will have its intended consequence . . . Policies based upon incorrect assumptions probably will not work and may well have unintended (possibly undesirable) consequences.[3]

Wise may have gone too far in suggesting that assumptions may be 'correct' rather than appropriate or intelligent. The genesis of curriculum theory as prescription is of course related to the broader social and economic context into which schooling is placed in Western countries. Particularly under US influence (where many of the first attempts to provide theories of curriculum arose), the emphasis has been on providing *rational* and *scientific* modes of curriculum design and implementation. Operating a rational model of 'scientific management' in education demands that curriculum theorists offer maximum help in the defining of objectives and programmes.

Wirth has characterized this American model of curriculum management in the following manner, arguing that 'in the 1960s and 70s we witnessed a transformation of American schooling by technocratic ideology and systems analysis techniques – the sophisticated successor to Taylorist social efficiency practices of the early twentieth century':

> Believers in the new technocratic ideology hold to a faith that a systems analysis approach which produces airplanes will also produce efficient child learning, and to belief in a crude form of behaviourism which assumes that behaviours will occur if it is specified that they shall occur. They assume that the principles of a mechanical model of production and cost/benefit economic principles can be transferred to education. The intention is to conceive of a science of education analogous to the sciences of mechanical production.[4]

Given the predominance of the existing political and economic order and associated ideologies (particularly since the 'end of history' was pronounced), it thus becomes clear in which direction curriculum theorists will be steered. The theorists' task will be to provide a range of objectives for the system to sponsor, test and achieve. In addition, a 'science of education' is required to underpin scientific management of the system. The management imperative and the support it offers in maintaining the legitimacy and control of the status quo is clearly in evidence. 'To true believers in educational results by "scientific efficiency" and bureaucratic social controls, the rationalistic model of schooling . . . is unquestionably correct. If the schools are given clear, measurable objectives, the objectives will be met.' For Wise, the model gains its force and legitimacy from its origins in the factory. He says that the

> policy making process has an affinity for a rationalistic conception of teaching and the teacher. The reasons are simple: The will of the policy maker must be implemented; the expectations for what the schools are to accomplish must be translated into action; the workers (teachers) in the factory (school) must perform their assigned tasks and the bureaucracy must be peopled by bureaucrats who will implement the official goals of the institution.[5]

There are, however, dangers in writing with the power of hindsight. For the moment the tendency outlined may be dominant and it has always been massively powerful. Yet we must remember that in the 1960s and early 1970s a range of contradictory tendencies were also evident, sometimes influentially. To explain the overwhelming influence of prescriptive curriculum theories we need also to analyse the previous responses of those educators with a more sensitive appreciation of the educational enterprise. Why was it that those who did, and do, oppose the simplifications of rationalism and scientism either were coopted to prescriptive curriculum theories or, more often, abandoned theorizing altogether?

The explanation, I believe, turns on a sad irony. Those educators and curriculum theorists who opposed the reductionism of scientific management counterposed a view of education as potentially liberating and exciting. They were, in short, concerned to build an improved world. Above all they wanted to be involved in *action*, not theory. They believed their action would have fundamental and long-lasting effect. Analysis of what was already in schools was therefore mere archaeology, and theorizing if there was a need for it could come later: after the curriculum revolution. This response to existing practice and theory has happened in previous periods of flux in curriculum. Kliebard tells us that in the United States in the 1920s the curriculum reformers almost totally rejected earlier established procedures and practices, which they generally associated with the discredited doctrine of mental discipline. 'The belief in change now was sufficient to argue for transcending all past notions of theory and of practice. The ambivalence to research and theory is particularly significant.'

> In the curriculum field . . . the urge to do good is so immediate, so direct, and so overwhelming that there has been virtually no toleration of the kind of long-range research that has little immediate value to practitioners in the field, but which may in the long run contribute significantly to our basic knowledge and understanding.[6]

Westbury some time ago identified this *meliorist* tendency along with its implications for curriculum theorizing:

> A vision can so easily slide into meliorism and, unfortunately, the consequences of such a meliorist perspective have long beset our field: too often and for too much of our history we have not been able, because of our commitment to what should be, to look at what is. To look at what is betrays, our emphases suggest, too little passion, even perhaps a conservative willingness to accept schools as they are. Indeed, all too often our stances imply a condemnation of what schools do.[7]

In later sections I develop further the argument that a major stumbling block in effecting change in the 1960s and 1970s was our arrogance in initiating change from above and beyond without sufficient analysis of what was already there. But again a sense of historical period is a major part of the explanation for these failings. It is now difficult to reconstruct the optimism and commitment of curriculum debate and reform initiatives at that time. But the documents give testimony to a widespread belief that schooling was about to change in fundamental and revolutionary ways. One is reminded of Clancy Segal's description of California in the mid-1960s: 'Each moment of the present promised so much of the future that the past seemed irrelevant.'[8] Hence the times gave support to an ahistorical view of curriculum theorizing and action, to a belief that the focus was rightly on 'what should be rather than what is'.

A further reason for the ambivalence to curriculum theory might be added. I believe that a number of the more radical theorists actively embraced Trotsky's notion of 'impossibilism'. The point was to prescribe impossible goals for teachers (and pupils) to achieve in school. That way, so the argument proceeds, they will come to embrace the real 'truth', which is that the system can never – by its very structure and intentions – meet their needs. This moves the struggle closer to the day of actual revolt. Reid has characterized the radical theorist in this manner:

> The theorist is aware of problems of 'hidden curricula' of purposes and processes that lie behind the calls for the achievement of objectives or for the extension of the claims of systems over individuals. But his response is either to remove himself to a higher moral and intellectual plane from which he can safely criticise those who actually get involved in the practical curriculum tasks, or to declare that the only way of being involved in the improvement of curricula is to work for social revolution (usually in a Marxist sense).[9]

But this was only one tendency within the radical critique; as we shall see later, other radical tendencies were to help in pioneering new and valuable approaches.

To summarize: the mode of curriculum theorizing that has dominated the field is rationalistic and closely aligned to modes of scientific management and analysis; curriculum theories are essentially prescriptions. Ironically those who have sought to counteract these tendencies have failed to present a coherent alternative mode of theorizing; above all they have been concerned with curriculum action. In the former case we have a logical pursuit of a political (and educational) view. In the latter case, I shall argue, the ambivalence to theorizing is a betrayal of the cause. Meliorism (and indeed impossibilism) do violence to the complexities of educational practice; sometimes for the best of reasons they have led to a simplistic and ahistorical view of process. In their different ways both the prescriptive theorists and those with an action orientation have ignored what *is* in pursuit of what *might be*. It is time both came to grips with the ongoing realities from which all sides seem to be in full flight.

Underpinning curriculum theory as prescription

In analysing what underpins prescriptive modes of theorizing there is clearly a range of locations where one might begin. In the case studies that follow I focus on one aspect of what *is* in curriculum: the school subject. Hence in this section I want to examine the theories and definitions of objectives as they relate to school subject knowledge. By concentrating on one aspect of curriculum in this manner it may be possible to elucidate further the way in which prescriptive theory originates and operates.

While psychological theory may have been a general support, particularly in the scientific management structures discussed in the first section, philosophy has been of undoubted import with respect to the social construction and definition of school subjects. I do not at this point want to intrude too far on the debate between the philosophical absolutists and social relativists: plainly a dialogue of the deaf. My concern is rather to characterize the implicit *posture* of philosophy with regard to the school curriculum.

At its heart, philosophy seems to hold itself well above the fray of curriculum as existing and as currently realized. The core of this aloofness is a commitment to rational and logical pursuit. But the other side of the coin is a resistance to the force of social influence. It is as if the philosopher searches for truths *beyond* social interference. This is true of even the more liberal philosophers. Take Hirst, for instance. Objective knowledge, he says, 'is a form of education knowing no limits other than those necessarily imposed by the nature of rational knowledge and thereby developing in man the final court of appeal in all human affairs.'[10] Or take Pring: Forms of knowledge therefore are fundamental structures picked out by characteristic conceps and characteristic tests of truth. They are not options open to us; they constitute what it *means* to think and they characterise all our particular judgements.'[11] The 'philosopher king' knows only 'truth' then; there are no options for they have access to a truth beyond culture and beyond history.

At a certain level of discourse this may well be a sustainable position. But facing the process of teaching forms of knowledge are we still in a position where 'they are not options open to us'? On this point some of the philosophers show signs of almost human ambivalence. Others, however, have the strength of their convictions. Phenix, for instance, deliberately equates the disciplines with teachability: 'My theme has been that the curriculum should consist entirely of knowledge which comes from the disciplines, for the reason that the disciplines reveal knowledge in its teachable forms.'[12] Phenix's statement reveals, I think, the likely policy outcome of the more recently dominant philosophical mode of theorizing. Whatever the qualifications, whatever the studied detachment, the likely effect of the posture will be prescriptive theorizing. From a certainty that 'there are no options' it is clear that prescriptive objectives for schooling will be both the expectation and the culmination.

The extent to which philosophy has in fact contributed to prescriptive theorizing can be seen in a wide range of curriculum books for specialists of all kinds, the work of Bruner and Phenix in the United States through to Lawton and Peters in the United Kingdom. Lawton is a particularly useful example of how the curriculum specialist receives the messages of the philosopher. Lawton argues that, for Hirst, 'the theory seems to me to run as follows: the first principle is that we should be clear about our educational goals.' The second is that 'the central objectives of education are developments of the mind.' He adds later:

I have included Hirst's viewpoint here as an example of curriculum planning which is largely 'non-cultural' in the sense of being transcultural.

This is because Hirst sees the curriculum largely in terms of knowledge, and the structure and organisation of knowledge is, by his analysis, universal rather than culturally based.[13]

Philosophy then leads us beyond culture and above all leads to curriculum theories that allow us to 'be clear about our educational goals'.

However, the believers in educational goals based on the disciplines have ultimately to face the sad truth that the world of schooling as it currently exists is played on a pitch where scoring goals is difficult and the goalposts are not always relevant. There is a tearful little section in Lawton headed 'Disciplines but not subjects'. Here the confrontation between philosophical and prescriptive truth and curriculum reality leads to peculiar paroxysms to escape culpability for the prescription's failures. Hence Lawton writes:

> there is no reason why a curriculum based on disciplines should not be related to the children's own experience and interests. The fact that so much so-called academic teaching of subjects does tend to neglect children's everyday knowledge . . . is a condemnation of traditional pedagogy or teaching-method rather than disciplines themselves as a basis of the curriculum.[14]

One wonders what a philosopher would make of the logic of culpability here (are the disciplines beyond logic as well as culture?).

This is to do less than justice to Lawton or Hirst. Both these writers have shown considerable sensitivity to the problems of curriculum change and implementation. I have pursued the point to show that even sophisticated theorists are on the horns of a dilemma when working within the prescriptive mode. Hirst has pronounced at length on the dilemma in his article 'The forms of knowledge revisited':

> The importance of the disciplines, in the various senses distinguished, for school education, must not be minimised. What matters in this discussion is that the logical priority of intellectual objectives be recognised even if in terms of wider human values they are sometimes judged secondary. Equally their logical structure cannot be denied if they are ever to be attained. The concerns of the universities mean that their organisations of teaching and research necessarily embody these concerns to a high degree. But schools are not universities and their teaching functions are significantly different. These need to be seen in their own right for what they are. And if once that is done then not only do the disciplines matter, but many other things matter as well, things of major psychological and social concern which must not be over-looked.

This leads to a final epilogue for the forms of knowledge as prescriptions: 'Education is a complex business and philosophical analysis can contribute to our planning of it in a limited way. What it can do is alert us to the danger of too easy decisions and the issue of the place of the disciplines is more than a philosophical affair. What more there is to it, I must however leave to others.'[15]

The humility of this epilogue is both appealing and a clear statement of how limited the aspirations of the philosopher have become. But several logical steps are still missing before we arrive at this denouement. It is all very well to leave it to others. But who? It is all very well to alert us to the danger of easy decision. But what if philosophy has led to the very dangers of prescriptive simplicities to which we have drawn attention? To go back even further, if schools and teaching need to be seen for what they are, why does the analysis not start there? We are left with a basic message. If curriculum theory is to be of use it must *begin* with studies which *observe* schools and teaching. Our theory must grow from a developed understanding of the curriculum as it is produced and realized and of how, over time, this has been reproduced. We need, in short, not theories of curriculum prescriptions but studies, and eventually theories, of curriculum production and realization.

The reaction to alienated theory

As was noted in the first section an important counter-tendency was evident within the curriculum field in the 1960s and 1970s. There was a reaction to the simplifications, indeed abdications, of the rational, scientific school of curriculum theory, but one which was heavily laden with meliorist (or even impossibilist) tendencies.

At the centre of the reaction was knowledge of the complexity of the educational enterprise of which Hirst wrote. This makes the pursuit of a 'science of education' utterly illusory and, as Goodlad has noted, this is of great significance for those pursuing scientific prescriptions: 'There is not a science of education sufficient to give credence to the scientism necessarily indicated if any model of accountability . . . is to function effectively. It is an idea whose time has not yet come, whatever rhetorical and political support it is able to muster.'[16] Ernest House has made a similar point in 'Evaluation as scientific management in US school reform':

> The systems analysis approach to evaluation promises to substitute specific techniques derived from 'science' for the knowledge of craft in teaching. It is a false promise, for such simple techniques cannot substitute for full fledged professional knowledge, much of it tacit rather than explicit, which has been acquired over many years. Such a technological vision of knowledge rests on a confusion of tacit knowledge with generalisations and rules of procedure. In teaching as in speaking, if one relied on the formalised, externalised rules of procedure, one would be mute. The challenge for evaluation then is to arrive at approaches which are complementary to professional craft and which sharpen actual practice rather than those which threatened to replace practice.[17]

In the 1960s and 1970s the distinction between theory and practice often led to a reaction against theory *per se* not to a reformulation of theory. Theory as constituted, as we have seen, merely collides with curriculum reality. The collision left the theorists fairly overtly at a loss – 'we'd better leave this to others'. But the 'others' who were more immersed in the reality of curriculum production and operation drew their own conclusions about theory. If it had so little to say about the reality of practice, if in fact it grievously misrepresented or even 'threatened to replace' practice, was it not best to do without theory altogether or at least leave theorizing until later?

The response in the curriculum field strongly echoes the pendulum swings in sociology at about the same time. The pre-eminent positivist enterprise employed a scientific hypothetico-deductive model. The aim was to discover the social laws which underpinned everyday reality. Above all they followed a model related to the philosophy of science, which had as its major objective the seeking of objective facts about the social world. The scientist seeks a knowledge of the social system separate from and beyond the perceptions of the people who inhabit that system, pursuing wide-ranging laws and truth.

The reaction to this pursuit of scientific and universalistic laws came from symbolic interactionists, ethno-methodologists and sociologists of knowledge arguing for the rehabilitation of 'man' himself and his subjective perceptions and 'constructions' of reality. Drawing on Weber and Mead we had the work of Schutz, Goffman and Berger and Luckmann. The latter were characteristic in arguing that 'common sense knowledge rather than ideas must be the central focus for the sociology of knowledge. It is precisely this knowledge that constitutes the fabric of meanings without which no society can exist.'[18]

The stress on subjective perceptions in sociology engendered substantial responses in the curriculum field. Ambivalence about theory, the manifest lack of fit with practice, caused the pendulum to swing wildly when the reaction began. One of the leaders, Joseph Schwab, sought to rehabilitate 'the practical' in reaction to incompetent theory. Writing in 1970 (interestingly the same year as the Centre for *Applied* Research in Education began in England), Schwab took an apocalyptic stance:

> The field of curriculum is moribund. It is unable, by its present methods and principles, to continue its work and contribute significantly to the advancement of education. It requires new principles which will generate a new view of the character and variety of its problems. It requires new methods appropriate to the new budget of problems.[19]

Schwab was absolutely clear why the curriculum field was moribund. His indictment is plain and powerful:

> The curriculum field has reached this unhappy state by inveterate, unexamined, and mistaken reliance on *theory*. On the one hand it has adopted theories (from outside the field of education) concerning ethics, knowledge, political and social structure, learning, mind, and personality, and has used these borrowed theories theoretically, i.e. as principles from which to 'deduce' right aims and procedures for schools and classrooms. On the other hand, it has attempted construction of educational theories, particularly theories of curriculum and instruction.

Schwab then lists the 'grave difficulties (incoherence of the curriculum, failure and discontinuity in actual schooling)' to which theoretical activities have led. This is because

> theoretical constructions are, in the main, ill-fitted and inappropriate to problems of actual teaching and learning. Theory, by its very character, does not and cannot take account of all the matters which are crucial to questions of what, who, and how to teach: that is, theories cannot be applied as principles to the solution of problems concerning what to do with or for real individuals, small groups, or real institutions located in time and space – the subjects and clients of schooling and schools.[20]

Above all then, Schwab wishes us to move away from the theoretical and embrace the practical. In terms of subject matter he juxtaposes the two options in this way: the theoretical is always something taken to be universal or pervasive and is investigated as if it were constant from instance to instance and impervious to changing circumstance. The practical, on the other hand, is always something taken as concrete and particular and treated as infinitely susceptible to circumstance, and therefore highly liable to unexpected change: 'this student, in that school, on the South side of Columbus, with Principal Jones during the present mayoralty of Ed Tweed and in view of the probability of his re-election'.

In the United Kingdom the rehabilitation of the practice and process of schooling followed similar lines, echoing the new trends in sociology and certain tendencies, not only Schwabian, within American curriculum studies. A wide range of ethnographic and interactionist studies emerged, focusing on the process of social stratification at the level of the school and the classroom. The Manchester School, in particular Hargreaves, Lacey and Lambart, adopted an approach with antecedents in anthropology. The commitment was to trying to understand how teachers and pupils 'constructed' the world of the school. Without detailed study of the school, progress was impossible. While they were not primarily concerned with curriculum issues their academic leadership led to a more applied approach in curriculum research.

One centre that took a lead in applied work was the Centre for Applied Research in Education (CARE) at the University of East Anglia. CARE was founded in 1970 and embraced commitment to the teacher and his or her perceptions and constructions. The wide range of publications produced allow us to analyse the intentions and positions of those working at CARE. While claims can be made for the uniqueness of CARE there is much that is symptomatic and typical of beliefs at the time. If we look in some detail at CARE it may then be possible to understand some of the reasons for the posture adopted by leading curriculum developers during this period.

In his influential book *An Introduction to Curriculum Research and Development*, Lawrence Stenhouse stated that it is the thesis of the book that 'curriculum development must rest on teacher development and that it should promote it and hence the professionalism of the teacher. Curriculum development translates ideas into classroom practicalities and thereby helps the teacher to strengthen his practice by systematically and thoughtfully testing ideas.'[21] The stress on classroom practicalities echoes Schwab and became a strongly held value position at CARE. Working as a teacher at the time, in contact with a number of CARE personnel including Stenhouse, MacDonald and Walker, I was a beneficiary of their commitment and, quite literally, care. Walker, with whom I have worked especially closely on projects and articles, and to whom my debt is substantial, put the posture with regard to curriculum studies in this way. The work, he argued, 'would start with, and remain close to, the common-sense knowledge of the practitioner, and the constraints within which he works. It would aim to systematise and to build on practitioners' lore rather than supplant it.'[22] Barton and Lawn have commented that

> In separating 'pure' from 'applied' research, Walker feels he has suc-cessfully rid himself of a theoretical stance and, moreover, reduced the isolation of the researcher. What now counts for him is not a theoretical understanding of any particular situation but the understanding and self-recognition he can give his subjects.[23]

On the latter point I can certainly testify but the points on the aversion to theory are, I think, substantial, and the authors go on to claim that 'CARE's aversion to theory and to theorising is consistent throughout its membership . . . the question often appears to be a choice between theory and truth.'

Of course from the critique presented herein of curriculum theory the latter point is well taken. The danger, however, is that the reaction to prescriptive theory had led to a full flight from theory *per se*. There is substantial evidence of this happening at CARE in the 1970s.[24]

The significance of the CARE position, in articulating this strong 'action' and practice position, is that it was symptomatic of a major counter-tendency in the curriculum field at the time – spreading throughout the new 'applied research' to 'action-research' and pervading case study, ethnography and inter-actionist studies of classrooms and evaluation. Macdonald, the *éminence grise* of British evaluation, once broke cover to explain why his view of evaluation was thus, above all, in reaction to controlling theories of 'cost benefit' and 'manage-ment by objectives': 'The tendency of language like this is to suggest that the production of educated people is much like the production of anything else, a technological problem of specification and manufacture.'[25]

The reasons for the reaction to theory are clear but it was, one must remem-ber, a reaction to a particular kind of prescriptive theory suiting the ideological and economic context in which it was produced. The pendulum swing pro-duced a full-scale flight to the arena of action, of practice, the classroom, the practitioner, the practical. We stand witness to a celebration of the practical, a revolt against the abstract. We are back with Rousseau and Emile.

The problem of the hasty embrace of action and practice was compounded by the kind of action embraced. To the problems of the methodology of action and practical specificity must be added the problem of *focus*. Not surprisingly, those with a strong belief in practice and action sought ways of becoming involved. Curriculum projects offered a way into curriculum action: the ethos of CARE developed from the involvement of the key personnel in the preceding Humanities Curriculum Project (HCP). The particular view of professionalism and politics developed on HCP was later transferred over to become a position about curriculum research in general.

In the 1960s and the early part of the 1970s a wide range of curriculum research studies and papers discussed the issue of curriculum change. It was always dealt with as synonymous with *innovation*. Eric Hoyle's '*How does the curriculum change: a proposal for inquiries*' is a good example.[26] In addition, innovation and curriculum projects were viewed as synonymous. To confirm the point it is worth re-reading Parlett and Hamilton's important paper on *evaluation as illumination*. The specificity of focus for those seeking to change the school curriculum is clear. The illuminative evaluator was characteristically concerned with 'what is happening'. They therefore wanted to 'Study the innovatory project: how it operates, how it is influenced by the various school situations in which it is applied; what those directly concerned regard as it's advantages and disadvantages and how students' intellectual tasks and academic experiences are more affected.' The illuminative evaluator then 'aims to discover and document what it is like to be participating in the scheme, whether as a teacher or pupil; and in addition, to discern and discuss the innovation's most significant features, recurring concomitants and critical processes.'[27]

So a major milieu for those reacting to the rational/scientific school of prescriptive theorizing, given the terrain of the 1960s and 1970s curriculum field, was the innovative curriculum project. Those projects in a sense offered a perfect milieu for those with an ambivalence or antipathy to theory and a wish to be immersed in the day-to-day realities of practice and action. The problem, however, was not that it offered immersion in the milieu of action but that it was immersion in very *specific* milieu of action. This allowed project staff initially to have it both ways. There was no need for the generalizability of theories or programmes, for the project normally centred on a limited number of chosen 'pilot' schools. The need for theory could be easily and justifiably suspended.

The problems began when projects sought to generalize their work: the move, if you like, from the pilot stage towards new mainstream structures. Here though, beginning from the opposite starting point, the projects often responded with the very prescriptions and programmes they had reacted against. There were prescriptions of idealized practice, like the 'neutral chairman'; modules and courses, like 'Man: a Course of Study'; and new materials and curriculum packages. The prescriptions were buttressed with more theoretical pronouncements, with stark similarity to the prescriptive theories they had reacted against. There were now RDD models (research, development, dissemination) or KPU models (knowledge, production and utilization).

The sad truth was that starting from utterly different points prescriptive theory and immersion in practice led to the same collision point: everyday classroom life and existing syllabuses, exams, subject structures and subject communities. Again the posture ended up as exhortation, or 'we must leave this to others'. Take my comments from some time ago on the History 13–16 project, one of the more thoughtfully conceived and executed projects:

History 13–16 has a very impressive record; large numbers of guides and materials have been produced and meetings and conferences held. The thorny problems of examination and pedagogic style have been consistently confronted. Significant numbers of schools are now teaching the new history syllabus. In a real sense the project has done all that could have been expected of it.

The major weakness of the project is one common to most curriculum reform movements and projects, namely, the strategies for achieving basic change in classroom pedagogy. Such change has proved enormously difficult to encourage because of the range of constraints which persuade teachers to transmit factual knowledge to more or less passive students. 'Active learning situations', where the teacher ceases being merely a transmitter of facts, are certainly far more elusive than the implementing strategies drawn up by the project ever hint at.

The project hardly offers a coherent scheme at this level; more a mixture of laissez-faire and hope. The former is illustrated by comments about how to deal with third-form history: 'It is a problem which most teachers must work out for themselves, in the light of the differing circumstances in which they are placed'.

Hope is evident in a range of statements. The strategy for getting teachers to use more evidence was described in this way: 'The project hopes to give teachers a rationale for making evidence central to history teaching and also give to them, by the production of materials, some of the tools for the job'.

Fundamentally the project's hopes seem to have been for a change in pedagogy through *exhortation*. This is well illustrated by the attempts to get teachers to use discussion methods: 'Teachers will need to be willing to discuss with pupils their own reasons for teaching history and for seeing it as useful educative for adolescents'.[28]

In seeking to change classroom pedagogy a curriculum project is approaching one of the vested traditions within teaching and one supported by a huge range of rational and irrational arguments. Traditional teaching patterns have not and will not be changed by exhortation or by *new* materials that can be readily put to use in teaching with the *old* method.[29]

The comments are so reminiscent of the impotence of prescriptive curriculum theory; instead of problems 'to be left to others' we have problems 'teachers must work out for themselves, in the light of the differing circumstances in which they are placed'.

The point of previous abdication, it now should be clear, must become our starting point. Curriculum research and theory must begin by investigating how the curriculum is currently constructed and then produced by teachers in the 'differing circumstances in which they are placed'. Moreover, our theory needs to move towards how those circumstances are not just 'placed' but systematically constructed; for the persistence of styles of practice is partly the result of the construction of persistent circumstances.

We need to begin by understanding how curriculum is currently produced and why matters operate in the way they do. In short, we need a theory of context that underpins action. In such a manner a new curriculum initiative or project would pilot not so much materials as policy. The negotiation of new 'circumstances' for practice, of new structures, would be part of the task in both theory and action.

As with industrial innovations and practices new initiatives in other countries often prove the best places to learn the lessons from previous waves of activity. For instance, some projects in Eire have drawn lessons from American and British undertakings. First they critically scrutinize previous curriculum models: 'The RDD and KPU model, looked at from the perspective of a number of systems and agencies, is no longer sustainable. Over the past few decades, such approaches have been seen not to work, except in most exceptional circumstances. A set of educational ideas cannot be developed and packaged for use at will.'[30] The need that is identified comes close to a theory of context. In the section on the Early School Leavers Project on organization for change we learn that

> It is good to see that organisational implications and consequences are of central concern to the Early School Leavers Project. General ideas are not enough: we must move towards an organisational framework to carry those ideas. However – and this is a serious problem – the structure that seems to be emerging – and has certainly emerged in England – is of a three-tiered kind, where the brightest, those geared for Higher Education, are in the top tier, while the potential dropouts are in the bottom. Is that really what we want? Do we want to see the alienated, the dispossessed on the bottom tier of such a structure? If we do not want it, can we nevertheless avoid it? Does consideration of the particular needs of a specific group – however large and politically ominous – necessarily commit us to a kind of educational and social stratification which many of us have been trying for years to scale down if not eliminate? Will our strategies at the stage of generalisation of these pilot studies take account of the consequences for school and society of this underlying trend?[31]

The essential point about these comments on context and structure is that they focus on the aspects which are least developed in both prescriptive theory and the reaction to it. The prescriptive mode assumes, and has assumed, that bureaucratic accountability and power can ensure implementation: the reaction has assumed that growth, optimism and ameliorism would complete the task. Neither was correct. Both modes abandoned the middle ground: existing and continuing practice and structures. Both modes shared a belief in transcending existing practice and structure. Both modes were quintessentially, sometimes explicitly, ahistorical.

This brings us back to a point made by Westbury: 'In all cases the curriculum can be seen as an *idea* that becomes a thing, an entity that has institutional and technical form.'[32] Taking these in turn: institutional form means curriculum is mediated by antecedent structures of status, syllabuses and subjects, by the professional groups and subgroups who inhabit existing curriculum territory; technical form means curriculum has to be translated from an idea into a technical specification, a teachable subject and an examinable syllabus. The achievement of high-status technical form will then relate to institutional form and the status attributed and resources distributed to the practitioner of curriculum.[33]

We are left requiring theories that pursue systematic investigation of how existing curricula originate, are reproduced, metamorphose and respond to new prescriptions; a theory, in short, of how people involved in the ongoing production and reproduction of curriculum act, react and interact. Put in this way it seems a tall order but there is important work already undertaken on which to build. The initial focus of future work has to be on the interest groups and structures that currently operate and frame curriculum. These are located in the middle ground between scientific/rational theories and Schwab's concrete and particular 'this student, in that school, on the South Side of Columbus'. It is on this middle ground that we need to focus our attention.

3 Curriculum History, Professionalization and the Social Organization of Knowledge

IVOR F. GOODSON WITH IAN R. DOWBIGGIN

One of the more striking trends within educational theory during recent years has been the growing interest in the history of the secondary school curriculum. This interest in curriculum history has perhaps been most visible in Great Britain and Australia, but there is evidence that it is gaining momentum in the USA, Canada and other parts of the world, thanks in part to the scholarly attention paid to recent historical studies of secondary school subjects.[1]

We maintain that this scholarly trend is a salutary one. It comes at a time when the possibilities for an extended paradigm of educational history are promising. This is not the first time that alternatives to mainstream history of education have been launched. In the 1960s and 1970s 'revisionism' generated a range of interesting studies throughout the Anglo-American world. But to many historians the appeal of 'revisionist' history of education is fading, largely as a result of dissatisfaction with the misuse of history to support broad sociopolitical interpretations or theories.[2] We too are critical of 'revisionist' approaches, but rather more because, like 'mainstream' history of education, they focus on the political and administrative contexts of schooling and remain 'external' to the school. Instead, we are concerned with penetrating the 'internal' patterns of schooling, but like the 'revisionists' we hold to the view that historical studies have a valuable role to play in challenging and informing theory. We contend that a shift to a historical paradigm grounded in the study of curriculum constitutes in many ways a return to scholarly initiatives launched some sixty years ago by academic educators in Britain, such as S. S. Laurie and Foster Watson.

A new yet complementary paradigm of curriculum history is particularly important because it enables us to scrutinize a fundamental part of schooling that historians have tended to ignore: the internal processes or 'black box' of the school. Curriculum history seeks to explain how school subjects, tracks and courses of study have constituted a mechanism to designate and differentiate students. It also offers a way to analyse the complex relations between school and society because it shows how schools both reflect and refract society's definitions of culturally valuable knowledge in ways that defy simplistic models of reproduction theory.

Our contention is that curriculum history has a further significance. We maintain that it enables us to examine the role that professions – like education – play in the social construction of knowledge.[3] Research into the social history of British secondary school subjects has shown how teachers have been encouraged to define their curricular knowledge in abstract, formal and scholarly terms in return for status, resources, territoriality and accreditation. A subtle yet pervasive series of incentives has compelled those educators eager to improve their professional prerogatives and credentials to surrender solicitously to the definitions of 'valuable knowledge' as formulated by university scholars. We need to know more about this historical process because of its obvious implications for present-day decisions regarding curricular policies and practice.

From a historiographic perspective, this issue is also important because it accords with recent studies in the history of other 'liberal' professions: for instance, nineteenth-century asylum psychiatry. In both cases subordinate groups of institutional practitioners voluntarily legitimized high-status patterns of knowledge by deferring to academic definitions of their working lives. The conclusion to be drawn is that hegemonic forms of knowledge are reinforced less through the one-dimensional process of 'socialization' than through the well-established connection between patterns of resource allocation and the associated work and career prospects these ensure.[4]

Our intention here is to review briefly what some recent research has revealed about the historical patterns followed by specific subjects in the British secondary school curriculum. We shall then compare this research and its findings with equally recent work done in the history of French psychiatric knowledge in the nineteenth century. Without minimizing the patent differences between secondary school teaching and public asylum psychiatry, we conclude that the history of both asylum mental medicine and secondary school subjects enables us to further our understanding of how professions become part of the bureaucratic organizations which shape social, political, economic and cultural life in the modern and postmodern eras. It shows that the more occupational groups and their representative associations have pursued the material incentives offered by the state, the more abstract and decontextualized professional knowledge has become. In the history of the British secondary curriculum, for example, the form of subject knowledge has grown increasingly irrelevant to the experience of learning, just as psychiatric knowledge in the nineteenth century grew increasingly irrelevant to effective therapy. The result is that formal knowledge has superseded practical and utilitarian knowledge as the central concern of professionals; as a result, possibilities for the care, cure, enlightenment and emancipation of client populations may have been displaced if not actually postponed.[5]

We maintain that historical studies which accept curriculum as a central factor of schooling will of necessity address these concerns. Yet the principal value of such work lies in its capacity to probe the internal reality and relative autonomy of schooling. Curriculum history views the school as something more than the simple instrument of ruling-class culture. It uncovers the traditions and legacies of school bureaucratic systems, those factors which prevent men and women from creating their own history under circumstances of their own choosing. It analyses the circumstances men and women experience as reality and explains how these have been negotiated, constructed and reconstructed over time. The work of curriculum scholars such as David Layton, Mary Waring and Harold Silver examines these internal processes of schooling and contributes to the eventual formulation of a dynamic model of how courses of study, pedagogy, finance, resources, selection and the economy intersect.[6]

I

In presenting the case for curriculum history, we shall briefly examine the history of biology and science education in late nineteenth- and twentieth-century Britain.[7] The history of these subjects leads to three general conclusions about the process of becoming a school subject, conclusions, we suggest, which have important implications for the historical study of other bodies of professional knowledge.

The first is that subjects are not monolithic entities but shifting amalgamations of subgroups and traditions which through contestation and compromise influence the direction of change. Second, the process of becoming a school subject features the evolution of the subject community from one promoting pedagogic and utilitarian purposes to one defining the subject as an academic 'discipline' with ties to university scholars. Third, the debate over curriculum can be interpreted in terms of conflict between subjects over status, resources and territory.

In addition, historical studies of secondary subjects in the British school curriculum disclose a steady shift from low-status marginality within the curriculum, through a utilitarian stage, and ultimately towards a definition of the subject as a 'discipline' with a rigid and rigorous body of knowledge. This evolution from one stage stressing content to another stressing form has been sustained by the close connection between academic status and resource allocation that is a fundamental feature of the British educational system, a connection whose origins can be traced to the examination system created by universities in the nineteenth century and codified in the School Certificate system in 1917. From this date the School Certificate and the university-controlled examination boards began to exert considerable influence over the secondary school curriculum. The effect of this influence has been that subjects seek to be recognized as examinable bodies of knowledge because this status means that they will have abler students, higher salaries, better staffing ratios, higher capitation allowances, more graded posts and generally better career prospects.

The history of biology as a school subject exemplifies this process of curricular change. In its pursuit of academic status it endorsed the control of university scholars over the subject. Initially, biology was overshadowed by botany and zoology during the nineteenth-century campaign to introduce scientific subjects into the secondary school curriculum. Yet with the discoveries in bacteriology, marine biology, physiological research and agricultural science in the latter years of the century, agencies like the British Association for the Advancement of Science, the British Social Hygiene Council and the Science Masters Association promoted the cause of biology as a school subject.

The twentieth century – particularly the interwar period – witnessed a growth in the utilitarian aspects of the subject as promoters argued that 'biology was capable of economic application and exploitation in industries such as fishing, agriculture, and forestry, and also in medicine.'[8] This strategy proved to be successful because during the course of the 1930s biology gained a foothold in the secondary school curriculum. By 1931 all eight examination boards had adopted biology as a school certificate examination. Yet these gains were offset by a growing disenchantment with the place occupied by advanced biological studies in schools. Complaints arose in the 1950s that biology was a subject for 'vocational training rather than . . . an instrument of education'.[9] Similarly, botany and zoology teachers in schools, reflecting the attitudes their university training tended to foster, resisted union. Consequently, biology was confined to the early years of the secondary school and to largely vocational training at O and A level.

This state of affairs sparked efforts in the 1960s to publicize a version of biology as a 'hard science' emphasizing laboratory experimentation and mathematical techniques. Laboratories were status symbols which tended to attract money and resources, especially from the Industrial Fund and from Nuffield Projects. As biology grew as a laboratory-based science in the universities, a new generation of biology graduates was trained, and the subject's incorporation as a high-status O and A level school subject was assured. At the same time, concerns surfaced at the height of biology's successes in the 1970s. Even though there was a strong body of current opinion that biology must outgrow its pedagogic and utilitarian origins and pursue status and resources through the promotion of the subject as a hard, experimental and rigorous science, there was an awareness that the subject's status as a scientific discipline was still vulnerable to calls from within and without the subject community for a more social and human teaching approach.

Therefore, biology followed a historical pattern which culminated in its becoming an academic discipline, a hard science, characterized by a body of knowledge whose content university specialist scholars selected. In return biology teachers received status, students and resources, which testified to their acceptance as purveyors of culturally valuable knowledge.

Historical studies of subjects like biology within the British secondary school sector point to a phenomenon which warrants more attention from historians of education generally. In Britain there was a discernible tendency in the history of school subjects to move away from an early stage when the content of the subject was oriented towards fulfilling practical and vocational aims. Because the material and professional conditions of school teaching were tied closely to its status as an examinable school subject ultimately defined by university specialist scholars, teachers were subtly encouraged to characterize their subject matter in ways that stressed academic and abstract features divorced from the interests and upbringing of most students. Indeed, the form and scholarly context of subject-knowledge grew more and more germane to the interests of teachers. School subject teachers gradually deserted their original concerns in the pursuit of professional objectives related to career and working conditions.

Perhaps no historical case study illustrates the conflict over the form of school subjects and exposes the hegemonic nature of academic knowledge as vividly as David Layton's account of 'the science of common things'. Largely the creation of the Victorian Richard Dawes, 'the science of common things' was a type of science education taught in some English elementary schools in the 1840s. Its subject-matter was secular and was drawn from 'things which interest [pupils] at present, as well as those likely to interest them in future – such as a description of their clothing, how it is manufactured, etc., the articles which they consume, from whence they come, the nature of the products of the parish which they themselves and those about them are helping to cultivate.'[10] Dawes's experiment in teaching 'scientific knowledge as it applied to an understanding of familiar things', in Layton's words, quickly proved to be successful and by the next decade seemed poised to become the most important version of science education within the elementary school curriculum.

However, this success was reversed during the 1850s, despite widespread official recognition of the effectiveness of 'the science of common things'. Physical science changed from a compulsory to an optional subject. The supply of trained science teachers dried up. In 1859 grants for science teaching were slashed and in 1862, with the Revised Code and 'payment by results', all specially targeted financial resources for science were withdrawn. The effect of these developments was to destroy systematically a successful early initiative in mass science education.

The conclusion to be drawn from the brief history of 'the science of common things' is that public schooling in Victorian Britain was being reconstructed and reorganized in a way which undermined real efforts to educate the lower orders. Support for this conclusion can be found in the parliamentary committee report of the British Association for the Advancement of Science. The committee had been set up in 1860 to examine which form of science education the upper classes required. For example, when confronted by the 'lucid and intelligent . . . reply' of a child who had taken 'the science of common things', the chairman expressed his admiration of 'the child's talents' but cautioned that 'It would be an unwholesome and vicious state of society in which those who are comparatively unblessed with nature's gifts should be generally superior in intellectual attainments to those above them in station.'[11]

When science eventually reappeared in the elementary school curriculum some twenty years later it was in a very different form from 'the science of common things'. A version of pure laboratory science had become accepted as the correct form of science, one which muted utilitarian purposes and stressed scholarship, research and enquiry for its own sake, and the differences between abstract scientific concepts and the world of everyday experience. As Brian Woolnough has argued, this tradition of grammar school science, with its rigid separation of scientific subjects, has proven to be particularly resilient despite recent attempts to stop this symbolic academic drift by introducing 'general science education'.[12]

The case study of 'the science of common things' demonstrates that in the history of science as a school subject there is a firm link between status and the definition of the subject as a pure laboratory science divorced from 'object teaching and nature study, with their pedagogical and utilitarian objectives'.[13] But this link derives largely from the emergence of laboratory research in universities, a process that, beginning in Europe in the last quarter of the nineteenth century, found its way to North American shores. In Canada, for example,

> By the mid-1920s the institutional structures that produced the university professor as a research-oriented professional were securely in place in Canadian universities. Though on a modest scale, university physicists as well as chemists and biologists could now develop their research programmes in harmony with their institutional setting. Graduate programmes provided them with students and the NRC provided grants and fellowships, as did the better endowed universities also. In this way a system of production of scientific knowledge, the output of which was publication, was set in motion.[14]

As the university definition of science grew in power and prestige in the twentieth century, the pressure on school science teachers to conform to scholarly criteria rather than respond to the immediate problems of teaching the subject effectively has grown apace. In other words, the type of science education represented by 'the science of common things' is at a distinct disadvantage in an age dominated by postsecondary opinions of what constitutes high-status and culturally valuable knowledge.

The history of British school subjects is significant not only for what it reveals about the bureaucratizing and professionalizing tendencies within public education in the modern era. It is also important because it shares striking similarities with the social history of psychiatry. By comparing the histories of curricular knowledge and psychiatric knowledge it is apparent that in both cases the context of professional practice is structured in ways which foster institutional ties with bureaucratic organizations whose hegemony in the definition of culturally valuable knowledge is difficult to counteract. Despite evidence of considerable professional resistance to this hegemonic pressure, the long-term outcome is the construction of bodies of knowledge which authorize a sharp dichotomy between professional prerogatives and the interests and needs of client groups. Of course, as William Reid has argued, following the insights of J. W. Meyer, professionals must be careful that this gap does not grow 'to the point where credibility collapses'. 'Nonetheless', to quote Reid, 'it remains true that what is important' for professional success 'is not the delivery of "goods" which can be publicly evaluated, but the development and maintenance of legitimating rhetorics which provide automatic support for correctly labelled activity.' With educators as well as psychiatrists, 'The choice of appropriate labels and the association of these in the public mind with plausible rhetorics of justification can be seen as the core mission.'[15] Historians who explore how professionals take such action will shed valuable light on the series of constraints and rewards which engender occupational styles of discourse that have limited practical usefulness for institutional populations.

II

Curriculum historians who address themselves to these issues can be heartened by the fact that scholars have identified similar gaps between knowledge and practice in the social history of science and medicine.[16] This conclusion is germane to the history of school subjects because it resembles what curriculum historians have discovered recently: that is, that the type of school knowledge found in curricula is chiefly important for its social value to teachers intent on pursuing professional rewards. The knowledge contained in medical theories, it appears, has fulfilled basically the same purpose.

The history of Western psychiatry in the nineteenth century confirms this hypothesis and also suggests that, like school subject knowledge, psychiatric knowledge tends to grow more formal, abstract and divorced from the context of patients' lives. This insight draws attention to the widening gap between the changing form and content of professional knowledge and the needs and interests of the clients/patients/pupils whom professionals were originally committed to serve.

The evidence indicates that the early nineteenth century origins of asylum psychiatry were generally characterized by a sincere commitment to the cure of mental patients. This era witnessed the introduction of the modern asylum, an institution self-consciously designed to provide a retreat through isolation from a disruptive, disorienting and often dissatisfying world.[17] The nineteenth-century asylum was based on the notion that this cloistered environment would, in conjunction with the activist intervention of a sympathetic practitioner, enable the individual patient to return to his or her senses and rejoin the outside world. It was also based on the optimistic belief that insanity could be cured, not through the use of drugs and other physicalist measures, but through a psychological approach called the 'moral treatment', a form of therapy which was addressed to the distinctive emotional needs of the individual patient.[18]

While the chronology was not the same for every nation, it is generally true that during the middle third of the nineteenth century things had begun to change. Trained physicians began to oust the talented lay or clerical amateurs who had been involved initially in the institutional treatment of the insane. As licensed doctors gradually took over administrative control of asylums, professional considerations overshadowed the relationship between therapists and patients. Because the patient population was growing beyond the capacity of physicians to minister to individual patients, many doctors in mental hospitals found their time and energy increasingly devoted to administrative and managerial matters.

Thus, the difficulties in practising 'moral treatment' in asylums encouraged many physicians to concentrate on improving their dissatisfying professional circumstances. Psychiatrists in the middle third of the century looked increasingly to the state to build more asylums, hence providing better employment opportunities. In France, in particular, psychiatrists urged the government to centralize the national asylum system by establishing uniform standards for pay, promotion, pensions and working conditions. They also encouraged the government to end the long-standing division of powers between doctors and laypeople or clerics by making physicians the lone authorities in the management and administration of mental hospitals.[19]

None the less, there were still some psychiatrists who remained wedded to the original ethos of the modern asylum and refused to renounce the therapeutic optimism, psychological approach and suspicion of theory which had characterized the early years of the century. Just as subject groups are not monolithic entities but actually shifting amalgamations of competing subgroups, so psychiatry in the middle third of the century embraced both this trend and a group who began to advocate a more biologically oriented approach to the interpretation of mental illness as a way of improving the profession's image of expertise and specialized knowledge.[20] This latter group felt that as long as mental disease was viewed as little more than a disorder of pure mind, there would be no way of plausibly justifying the sole intervention of physicians in the institutional treatment of insanity.

Symptomatic of this tension within mental medicine was the founding of psychiatric associations in France, Britain and the USA in the 1840s and 1850s. The appearance of these organizations – like the formation of subject associations – indicated that asylum physicians wished to unify the profession's subgroups in order better to pursue professional interests.

By the final third of the nineteenth century, it was becoming clear that the faction within psychiatry in favour of a more biological or organicist orientation was gaining sway. The principal reason for the psychiatric swing away from a largely psychological approach to therapy and theory towards a more somatic and naturalist orientation was the psychiatric awareness that improved resources and career opportunities for asylum medicine hinged on its capacity to convince the state that it was a corps of expert practitioners privy to a scholarly and scientific body of medical knowledge; in other words, something more than 'moral entrepreneurs', to use Eliot Friedson's term.[21]

Throughout the Western world – but especially in France – this psychiatric strategy often took the form of adherence to the hereditarian theory of degeneracy in the final third of the nineteenth century.[22] But psychiatrists also stressed the positivist qualities of psychiatric knowledge, maintaining that, by relating the most recent discoveries in the anatomy and physiology of the brain to the clinical observation of pathological mental symptoms, psychiatry had ceased to be a chiefly psychological endeavour. By following the 'positivist method' of studying the anatomy and physiology of the brain and the factors that cause it to malfunction, French psychiatrists in particular hoped to improve their academic status and end the subservience to their patients which they felt they endured as long as they were viewed simply as 'mad-doctors' and 'alienists'.[23]

The growing attraction to psychiatrists of degeneracy theory, positivism and somaticism during the final decades of the nineteenth century indicated that doctors of psychological medicine were intent on creating the impression that as purveyors of esoteric and scientific knowledge they were entitled to the academic status that accompanied official recognition as a medical specialty by university faculties of medicine. This process was perhaps most vividly evident in France, where psychiatrists were well aware that appeals to the cultural value of naturalist and scientific knowledge were congruent with the attitudes of leading republican politicians. The early 1880s was a time when successive republican governments officially and explicitly defended the advantages of positivism in their campaign to eliminate clerical involvement in the state educational system. The effect of this promotion of positivism was to make it virtually the hegemonic form of knowledge in late nineteenth-century France, and to encourage substantial investment in and a great expansion of science faculties in the state university system.[24] The 1870–90 period was also a time when concerted efforts were made to introduce in French medical faculties the German ideal of academic scientific activity based on laboratory research and scholarly publications. This led to reform of the medical school curriculum through the addition of subjects like physiology, anatomy, histology and microbiology. Reformers believed that this new model of academic scientific activity would substantially improve the prestige of academic medicine while 'increas[ing] the effectiveness of reformers' demands for greater academic freedom and larger budget allocations'.[25] In other words, when French psychiatrists exploited the rhetoric of positivism, they hoped to establish their specialty as a legitimate department within the university sector and as a bona fide part of the reformed curriculum at state faculties of medicine.

Behind this movement to shape psychiatric knowledge into a recognizably academic and scientific form was an aggressive psychiatric campaign to have chairs in the clinical study of mental and nervous diseases established at the state University Faculty of Medicine in Paris. A chair in mental pathology had been discontinued at the Faculty of Medicine in 1822 because of the left-wing political activism of students. From that date French psychiatrists had openly yearned for the re-establishment of this chair and the intellectual history of the profession had reflected this concern. When the new chairs were founded in 1877 and 1882 respectively it meant that the Faculty of Medicine would conduct official clinical courses in psychiatry at the university level.[26] More to the point, asylum psychiatry was now linked firmly to the state university system and its faculties of medicine, which, thanks to the considerable cultural and political status enjoyed by the natural and medical sciences during the Third Republic, enjoyed augmented autonomy and better students, salaries, buildings and laboratory facilities and equipment in the 1880s and 1890s.

The capacity of late nineteenth-century French psychiatry to depict itself as a medical specialty with bioscientific credentials was crucial, then, to the effort of psychological medicine to establish a foothold in the state university system and cover the tracks leading back to mental asylums and their institutionalized inmates. Not that this trend has gone unchallenged: periodically psychiatrists have argued that mental medicine ought to return to a form of practice which stressed the emotional needs of the patient. But as the twentieth century has witnessed the growth of university psychiatry, so the likely fate of these sporadic movements to jettison the 'biomedical model' of mental illness in favour of psychosocial explanations has been, if not predetermined, certainly highly prejudiced.

III

To summarize: like subject-knowledge in biology and science, psychiatric knowledge in the nineteenth century revealed a tendency to move beyond utilitarian and practical aims towards an academic and scholarly form which reflected high-status and hegemonic definitions of knowledge. The historical pattern followed by psychiatric knowledge symbolized an abandonment of the therapeutic and palliative needs of asylum patients and the pursuit of professional objectives whose realization, from the psychiatric perspective, was contingent upon closer ties with the state and the material advantages it could offer. Psychiatric knowledge eventually lost any relevance to the therapeutic imperatives of asylum physicians and thus became ossified and virtually useless for psychiatrists intent on the delivery of effective health care to their institutionalized patients.

Its advantages in other respects were considerable. It enabled psychiatry to stake a place for itself in the centralized university system, where psychiatrists could be taught and trained, and it authorized the process whereby the management and administration of public asylums would be placed solely in the hands of a trained and licensed physician. The academic and scholarly status that accompanied these achievements helped to convince the state that psychiatry warranted the resources which were fundamental to this professional survival and growth.

The resemblance between the history of psychiatric knowledge in the nineteenth century and the history of secondary school subjects indicates that they have undergone roughly the same 'morphology of reform', to borrow Carl Kaestle's terminology.[27] In both cases it is clear that knowledge increasingly became decontextualized and disembodied as the 'disciplines' developed closer and closer ties with the state and with university scholars. As high-status knowledge has been increasingly identified with the characteristics of scholarly knowledge generated and reinforced by university academics, there has been a growing perception that the material self-interests of professionals lie in the cultivation of a scholarly and academic image. Thus, professional knowledge tends to become more abstract and formal as occupational groups seek to gain footholds within the bureaucratic departments of the modern university. The evidence suggests that the trend towards more academic qualities is animated by the professional desire to acquire the mystique of specialization, which assures a monopoly of power, resources and prerogatives in a specific sphere of occupational practice. The price professions pay for these advantages is that they must defer to the 'kind of "education" that produces a system of special examinations' and whose form is ultimately defined by university scholars, not practitioners themselves.[28]

Our belief is that an extended paradigm which takes curriculum as its focal point will, by drawing attention to the actual participants in this complex historical process, enable scholars to explain why professionals comply with bureaucratic and corporate control of their occupational practice. In accounting for human process, it will shed light on the two levels of reality for historical actors: individual life-history and the experiences of specific groups or subgroups with interests in the organization of curricular knowledge. The ongoing negotiation of reality by both individuals and groups reveals the antecedent structures of power in education and suggests how the attitudes of dominant groups in society continue to influence schooling despite evidence of conflict and contestation. The political, social, economic and cultural debates over both schools and asylums have traditionally been heated and divisive, yet professional practice has been remarkably resistant to change. Curriculum historians who devote themselves to examining the emergence and survival of what we define as 'traditional' can do much to explain why schools have conformed to Kaestle's 'morphology of reform'. Perhaps their studies will also lead eventually to the formulation of theories and models which systematically investigate how existing curricula originate, are reproduced and respond to new prescriptions.

The 'traditional' link between academic status and patterns of resource allocation and career construction has been documented in the social history of British school subjects and the history of nineteenth-century French psychiatry. When scholars have further explored this issue, we shall know more about the internal nature of schooling, the forces which push and pull both teachers and students to reproduce or challenge the social structure outside schools. In recommending an extended paradigm for historical studies of education, we are not implying that the possibilities of other paradigms have been exhausted. Instead, we contend that a move towards curriculum history assumes that we analyse the administration and organization of educational structures and systems through a broader analysis of the enduring legacies of status, resources, curriculum and examination policy. We now need historical studies of education which encompass the study of structures as well as the other piece in the puzzle of educational change: the 'secret garden' of the curriculum. To date it has remained as secret to historians as to educational policy-makers.

4 Behind the Schoolhouse Door: The Historical Study of the Curriculum

IVOR F. GOODSON WITH CHRISTOPHER J. ANSTEAD

In April 1977 a group of educationists gathered at Teachers College, Columbia University, to consider forming an organization concerned with the study of the history of the curriculum. In particular, they wanted to attack 'the ahistorical and atheoretical character of curriculum reform efforts'.[1] Yet in the decade and a half that has elapsed, only slow progress has been made in closing the gap that exists between curriculum studies and history of education.

Any detailed analysis of curriculum stability and change demands an understanding of its history; any action-oriented theoretical enterprise ought first to consult the record of success and failure in the past. Curriculum specialists, however, seem reluctant to examine the past without the training imparted to professional historians. At the same time, the study of the history of education has tended to take an 'external' view of curriculum, focusing on political and administrative contexts and on general movements in education and schooling. Partly this is a reflection of the documents available, which often relate to central government regulations, edicts or commissions on education and curriculum. But this is a long way from curriculum as enacted, transacted, realized and received. Although more social and/or revisionist perspectives have gained in influence, especially in the past two decades, history of education, as institutionalized, has often retained a certain 'acts and facts' flavour. Histories of education that fail to analyse the internal nature of schooling merely accept the school as a 'black box', unopened and unanalysed, ignoring the vast potential for internal variety and change.

The reluctance of historians to look behind the schoolhouse door, and of curriculum specialists to use historical methods, serves as a drag on any attempt to comprehend schools and education. These are tendencies that must be overcome; in fact some writers are already working to do so. In an attempt to exemplify such work, this chapter concludes with an overview of one particular study of curriculum in its historical setting (see also Chapters 5 and 6). The plentiful sources of historical data discovered in this examination of a Canadian high school should encourage scholars to make the trip into the classroom more frequently. The rewards of the journey are abundant. This survey also outlines some of the historical methods and procedures used in the investigation – methods and procedures with which curriculum specialists should come to grips. It also raises some methodological problems which accompany such an undertaking, as caution for enthusiastic converts to historicism.

If the historical scrutiny of curriculum and curriculum change is to be given priority in contemporary studies of education, then a mode of enquiry that focuses on and analyses 'internal' issues in their historical context is of paramount importance. Partly, the crucial nature of internal factors results from the way education and schooling are structured and relate to the broader economy and society. As Webster has pointed out: 'Educational institutions are not as directly nor as essentially concerned with the economic and social welfare of the community as, say, factories or hospitals. They are, therefore, particularly well equipped to weather any crisis that may be going on around them.'[2] Although it is less and less the case as the 'free market' spreads its tentacles through the economic and social fabric, this relative autonomy has explained the peculiar force of historical traditions and legacies in curriculum change. As a result, as Waring reminds us, it is really not surprising that originality always works within the framework of tradition and that a totally new tradition is 'one of the most improbable of events'.[3]

Hence a sense of history will modify our view of curriculum. Instead of the transcendent expectation of basic change we might look for alteration followed by regression, for change attempted and aborted in one place to emerge unexpectedly elsewhere. Through history we develop a longer view and with it a different timescale of expectations and, presumably, range of strategies. The force of history is physically evident to any student of schooling and curriculum, in syllabuses, textbooks, school buildings and indeed school teachers – an overlay of generations, a time-lag of views, values and valedictions. Charlton warned that 'The present problem of curriculum planning is itself shot through with the past and with vestiges of the past, and future solutions however radical will inevitably carry something of the past with them.'[4] Likewise, Blumer has drawn attention to the problem when studying large-scale organizations, and argues a need 'to recognize that joint action is temporarily linked to previous joint action'. He warns that 'one shuts a major door to understanding any form or instance of joint action if one ignores this connection.'[5] If anything the need to understand the past traditions and legacies 'internal' to curriculum history is even more pressing in the spate of educational or neo-educational changes of the 1980s and 1990s.

Studies of historical events and periods are required in order to develop a cumulative understanding of the historical contexts in which the contemporary curriculum is embedded. In the past three decades we have seen the painful limitations of ahistorical or transcendent approaches at the level of both curriculum reform and study. Studies with an action-orientation have most often been confined to the view of participants at a moment in time, to the here and now of events. The essential omissions were data on the constraints beyond the lesson, the curricula, the school, the classroom and the participant. Although the human process by which people make their own history does not take place in circumstances of their own choosing, as men and women and circumstances do vary over time so too do the potentialities for negotiating reality. Historical study seeks to understand how thought and action have developed in past social circumstances. Following this development through time to the present affords insights into how those circumstances we experience as contemporary 'reality' have been negotiated, constructed and reconstructed over time. Stenhouse saw this need for 'history to provide an authenticated context for hypothetical actions'. His concern was also with 'What might be termed the contextual inertia within which events are embedded'.[6]

The historical context of course reflects previous patterns of contestation, conflict and power. But this in an inherently dynamic process; it is not sufficient to develop a static notion of the historical contexts and constraints inherited *in tacto* from the past. Contexts and constraints need to be examined in relationship to contemporary action. Moreover, we require a dynamic model of how curricula, pedagogy, finance, resources, selection and the economy all interrelate. We must avoid viewing the curriculum (and its associated historical contexts and constraints) as a bounded system. Williamson has reflected on the fact 'that it is not sufficient to be aware only of the fact that the principles governing the selection of transmittable knowledge reflect structures of power. It is essential to move beyond such suspicions to work out the precise connections'. This, he argues, predicates historical study of curriculum 'if the aim is to understand power in education'.[7] By placing one aspiration of curriculum history as elucidating the contextual background or immanent constraints on contemporary curriculum a number of conclusions follow. Where possible, curriculum history should also aim to scrutinize, test or contribute to educational theory. It is at the heart of the enterprise to examine curriculum development and transformation over time: such complex undertakings cannot be elucidated by 'snapshots' of unique historical events or periods. But the recurrence of events viewed in contemporary profile can help in discerning and examining explanatory frameworks and in understanding the manner in which structure and action interrelate. Curriculum history should be concerned, perhaps above all, with understanding the 'internal' process of curriculum definition, action and change because this is the least developed aspect of our scholarship. In due course this work must be relocated in the broader context of economic history and policy, but in ways that resonate with issues of relative institutional autonomy.

The study of historical context partly to illuminate the contemporary prospect implies a need to develop a dialogue between historians of education and curriculum specialists. It further implies a need for curriculum historians to accept a responsibility wherever possible to relate their work to contemporary situations and, again where possible, to develop theoretical insights and studies of internal process. Most certainly it means for any curriculum specialists undertaking the work that they must begin to learn and practise the skills of the historian. Why is it that those already trained in these skills have left this lacuna in the history of education? The answer arises from the historical context of history of education itself. In Britain and North America, the history of education has become institutionalized as 'acts and facts'.[8]

In England, teacher training first began systematically in the 1840s with the foundation of training colleges, of 'Queen's Scholarships' which contributed towards maintenance, and of examination certificates for trained adult teachers. In the beginning the training colleges focused on practice rather than theory.[9] While practical training predominated, a number of the colleges began to teach history of education in the last half of the nineteenth century. The teaching and the textbooks were normally provided by past schoolteachers rather than historical specialists.

From 1890 onwards 'university day training colleges' were established, following a minority report of the Cross Commission, which had recommended not just that teachers be trained in universities, but that faculties of education be established to initiate academic study and research in education. At first the universities provided three-year courses where the degree work and training for teaching were carried on alongside each other, merging theory and practice. Later theory and practice were made more separate, with work for the academic degree in the first three years and an additional year for practical professional training. Separate university departments of education began to be formed from 1911 onwards.

Similarly, teacher training in Canada and the United States started in the first half of the nineteenth century. At first most teachers took their professional education in normal schools – which provided an education equivalent to secondary schooling. By the turn of the century, though, teachers' colleges, offering work beyond secondary level, had become the institutional leaders in the field, eliminating normal schools completely by 1940. Starting in the last decades of the nineteenth century, and through most of the twentieth century, teacher education became a part of the university system as some universities opened faculties of education, others incorporated existing teachers' colleges, and many state teachers' colleges, especially in the American Midwest, became multipurpose state universities.[10]

As teacher educators asserted their place in postsecondary schooling, status concerns arose. At heart stood the theory–practice conundrum. Some teacher educators felt their whole purpose revolved around practical training in the art of teaching, while others – especially at university faculties of education – wished to emphasize theoretical study. Soon the most prestigious institutions – Teachers College, at Columbia, and the Schools of Education at Harvard and the University of Chicago – opted for a complete research orientation and ceased the training of beginning teachers.[11] When most schools of education bowed to the pressure to legitimate themselves in the eyes of their academic colleagues, history of education stood as 'the one area of educational research which at the time possessed a thoroughgoing, scholarly method of inquiry.'[12]

In Britain and North America, then, history of education became an important part of teacher preparation from the 1890s. But from the beginning these courses focused primarily on the history of educational institutions and systems and the history of educational theories and ideas – all taught in strict chronological sequence. Although a number of counter-tendencies developed in both mainstream history and the history of education, the predominance of 'acts and facts' courses lasted for a very long time.[13] Even in North America, where the 'social foundations' approach diluted history of education in a problem-solving social scientific framework, what remained of the subject in lectures was still focused on external factors.[14] The reasons for the dominance of 'acts and facts' history of education are numerous. Perhaps most important was the carry-over from the general mode of historical scholarship and writing at the time that history of education courses were devised and institutionalized in the colleges and university departments.[15] History as a discipline in the universities was growing quite rapidly at this time and was primarily concerned with national constitutional and political matters most often related in narrative manner.[16]

Although the specific social and political contexts of nineteenth-century Britain and North America contributed to this pattern, so did the associated range of documentary evidence on which history has to build its interpretations. Williams has reminded us that the problem of the 'selective tradition' is a general cultural phenomenon, which has a particular potency when practised by historians.

> To some extent, the selection begins within the period itself; from the whole body of activities, certain things are selected for value and emphasis. In general this selection will reflect the organisation of the period as a whole, though this does not mean that the values and emphases will later be confirmed. We see this clearly enough in the case of past periods, but we never really believe it about our own.[17]

For the historian the effects of contemporary selection and associated documentation are often conclusive. Historians of education who search out new areas of study therefore often collide with the intractable selections of past periods.[18]

These factors join with contemporary definitions of the relative importance of different types of historical problems to maintain history of education as a discipline that takes an external approach to schools. It is within schools, and, in particular, within classrooms, that the reality of curriculum delivery is negotiated; yet this is the one forum most neglected by historians of education. A few leaders in the field have pointed to this omission.[19] In 1986, Chad Gaffield called on Canadian historians of education to go 'back to school', and described the lack of any study of the classroom as 'a major weakness in the current historiography of education'.[20] Similarly, in early 1992 Harold Silver took American and British educational historians to task. According to Silver, in history of education as currently practised, 'There are no classrooms, no children, no teaching, no learning.'[21] He concludes: 'We have been writing the history of educational contexts, not of education.'[22]

Despite the foregoing, characterizing history of education in the past as predominantly 'acts and facts' is less than fair; as with any subject history of education has not been, and is not, monolithic. There have always been different, perhaps broader, visions at work within the subject. In seeking alternative paradigms for the historical study of education it is intriguing to return to the early work of the first professors of education, many of whom brought a conviction that historical studies could deepen an understanding of the educational terrain.[23]

The most systematic treatment of the history of the curriculum came from Foster Watson, who was appointed Professor of Education at the University College of Wales, Aberystwyth, in 1894. Watson's concern was to provide a detailed curriculum history and he argued for both its importance and, for its time, uniqueness:

> It will be generally admitted that it is high time that the historical facts with regard to the beginning of the teaching of modern subjects in England were known, and known in connection with the history of the social forces which brought them into the educational curriculum. This is precisely what is now attempted for the first time, as far as the writer knows, within a single volume.[24]

Regrettably, both in the specific case of launching curriculum history and in the general sense of launching a more broadly conceived view of history of education the work of the early professors was only pursued patchily in the twentieth century.

In the last quarter-century a growing literature, particularly from the USA, has sought to extend or critique this work, drawing inspiration from catalytic changes in mainstream history. Economic and social history have grown rapidly since the interwar years; oral history and feminist history have developed to try to exhume the 'invisible armies' suppressed by selective traditions; the work of Hobsbawm, Thompson, Genovese, Smith-Rosenberg and many others illustrates how such imposed selections can in fact be transcended; how the lived experiences in our culture can be reconstructed by historians.[25] These tendencies, which have been moulding the practice of history for decades, point to new possibilities for educational history. Perhaps the early promise of history of education courses as glimpsed by the first professors of education can at last be retrieved and carried on.

In fact, the past two decades have seen tremendous changes in the practice of history of education. Since 1970 or so, historians of education have carved out a professional niche for themselves in the academic field of mainstream history. They have linked up with the concerns of the dynamic social historians, leading to useful studies of education in terms of class, gender and ethnicity.[26] More recently, historians of education have followed their social history allies in turning away from studies of power structures, in favour of the examination of human responses to such structures, particularly in terms of the family.[27] Yet in their exuberant campaign to make their subject a subfield of social history, historians of education have distanced themselves from the topics of central concern to most members of education faculties.

There are already, however, a number of influential studies which do take up these concerns, represented in the UK by Waring's study of the *Nuffield Foundation Science Teaching Project*, and Harold Silver's essays in *Education as History*, in the USA by Labaree's examination of Philadelphia's Central High School and in Canada by Rowell and Gaskell's study of science curricula.[28] All this work shares a willingness where possible to develop links with contemporary curriculum and with educational theory and to examine and analyse 'internal' process. In the best of this work we have the painstaking reconstruction of a historical period and the development of an understanding of the connections between previous historical struggles and present contexts, actions and possibilities. We gain insights into the process of curriculum production.

In addition, a few historians of education have examined the actual process of education as it takes place within the classroom. One particularly fruitful area seems to be the work presently under way concerning teachers' lives and teachers' narratives. While this focus grew out of a concern with the impact of external forces – such as gender and class relations – on teachers, recent studies have moved into a broader consideration of the practice of teaching in a specific historical context. Larry Cuban deserves special credit here, while recent collections edited by Prentice and Theobald, and Goodson point to the strength of this new focus.[29] A few researchers have gone one step further and looked beyond the teacher to study the classroom as a whole. Short pieces by Tyack, Lowe and Hansot, and Sutherland provide the first glimpses of this approach.[30]

Having made the plea for more such studies, it is time for us to convince historians that the trip inside the schoolhouse is worthwhile, and to show curriculum specialists without a background in history how to start reviving the past. An examination in detail of the methods used by a current study might help to reassure the latter while showing the former the range of valuable data available. The rest of this chapter and the subsequent two chapters deal with a local study we are undertaking.

The case study in question involves an examination of the London Technical and Commercial High School (LTCHS) sited in London, Ontario, Canada. This study is not an institutional case history, but a study of school curricula set in a particular institution, at a particular time (1900–40). A further study beginning in 1993 will take us from 1940 to 1990. The project examines the nature of curriculum – its continuities and changes – at three levels. First, it examines the various course streams available at LTCHS. Second, its overall focus is on vocational education, which became popular in the progressive era, and which in London, Ontario, was synonymous with LTCHS. Finally, it travels through the schoolhouse door, to discover the ways in which teachers and students dealt with the curriculum as practised. As the study examines these examples of curriculum it deals with two major influences: professional concerns and external constituencies. The study also seeks to understand the effect of these curriculum patterns on students, especially in terms of stratification by class and gender. As an ongoing research project, the LTCHS study can provide certain insights. In particular, it can serve as an example of how one research team – originally consisting of Ivor Goodson and Ian Dowbiggin, and currently consisting of Goodson and Christopher Anstead – has attempted to use the methodological and evaluatory insights of historical research to study school curricula.

One major concern of researchers considering a historical study is the availability of sources; the LTCHS project found a wealth of evidence of different types. The school itself had maintained (more through inertia and ample storage space than any conscious plan) a large collection of documents relating to its early history. These included a complete run of the *Minutes* of the Advisory Vocational Committee – the body that supervised the school under the Board of Education. These minutes contained information on such mundane matters as school maintenance problems or the purchase of supplies, as well as information on the hiring, salaries and working conditions of teachers, and discussions regarding curriculum change in a broad sense. Of greatest value, though, were the long memoranda contributed by H. B. Beal, the school's principal and prime mover, which often included rhetorical discussion of the purpose of the school and its various departments.

Of equal value to the AVC *Minutes* were an almost complete run of student record cards from 1912 (the year the school opened) to 1935. The early cards listed a student's name, address, parental name and, after 1919, the course in which the student enrolled. After 1927 the cards included information on religion, date of birth, place of birth, parent's occupation and the student's occupational placement or reason for leaving, as well as a complete set of marks for every class taken. The cards allowed for an in-depth quantitative analysis to supplement the abundant qualitative sources.

Other official and administrative records available at the school included a scattered series of school mark books, teacher attendance logs and similar documents. Absent, though, was any information about what went on in the classroom. There were no notes on pedagogical practice or subject content, except in the most general terms.

Of course, any researcher or team is not bound by official records kept by the institution in question. In the case of the Beal school, a whole array of unofficial or official external records existed. Official external records included *Minutes* and *Annual Reports* of the Board of Education, as well as *Annual Reports* and other documents from the Ontario Ministry of Education. In written form, the chief unofficial source is the information contained in local newspapers, especially the *London Free Press*.

Several years ago, a group of teachers at the school decided to celebrate the institution's seventy-fifth anniversary by exploring some of its history. As a result, they established a depository of mementoes, now in virtually forgotten storage. This collection includes over a hundred photographs from the period before 1940, a classroom notebook from a cooking class in 1937 and a scrapbook started by H. B. Beal. The images in the photos and the notes in the notebook allow a first glimpse into the actual world of the classroom.

Beyond these readily available documents, the research team has decided actively to solicit oral testimonies and the loan of written sources from former students and teachers at the school. Sources such as diaries, letters and notebooks, which do not normally show up in school archives, allow a greater understanding of the school experience. Interviewing surviving teachers and students involves the researchers directly in the creation of new sources of historical evidence. The memories of these witnesses provide further information on classroom culture and pedagogical practice in the period. Of course, this source of information is not available to those studying nineteenth-century schooling.

Finally, one gap in the historical record emphasizes the way in which older selections privileged 'acts and facts' history. The Archives of Ontario contain all the material that still remains from the provincial Ministry of Education of this period. Before handing the material over to the Archives, ministerial bureaucrats sorted through it and discarded what they considered of little historical interest. Among the material discarded was anything related to the particular case of the LTCHS. While one side of correspondence between school and ministry is preserved in school sources, the other side of the conversation must remain forever silent. This underlines the point Alison Andrews makes:

> Documents have differential survival rates and those which do survive do not always provide all the information required. The fundamental difference between historical research and other forms of social enquiry is the impossibility of 'going back' to ask for further explanation and elaboration. This leads to all kinds of problems. The answers to a great many questions are simply not available, since the necessary records either never existed or failed to survive.[31]

To understand the historical sources that do remain, some reliance on the rules of the discipline of history both speeds the process and makes it more defensible. An axiom of historically based research states that evidence is useless without context; despite the critiques of those influenced by extreme postmodernism, this remains central to the interpretation of history.[32] As Mary Waring's work has argued,

> If we are to understand events, whether of thought or of action, knowledge of background is essential. Knowledge of events is merely the raw material of history: to be an intelligible reconstruction of the past, events must be related to other events, and to the assumptions and practices of the milieu. Hence they must be made the subject of inquiry, their origins as products of particular social and historical circumstance, the manner in which individuals and groups have acted must be identified, and explanations for their actions sought.[33]

Historical context consists of at least two dimensions – place and time. To understand what went on in LTCHS in the early twentieth century, the research team has to understand the early twentieth century in general; London, Ontario and Canada in general; and the history of education, especially curriculum, in general.

A different level of context comprises the theoretical expectations a researcher brings to her or his project. While one strong school of thought in historical research argues that a researcher should only address primary data after a survey of the secondary literature has led to the framing of a testable, theory-laden hypothesis, another school finds this approach abhorrent. More traditional historians object that theory-driven research prevents a researcher from approaching evidence with an open mind. This school prefers to start with the evidence and come up with interpretations out of it.

In the Beal project, we find strengths and weaknesses in each approach; our own methodology comprises an untidy mix of each, but we suspect that such a mix is not uncommon outside the boundaries of theoretical discourse. Thus we have approached the evidence only after reading widely in the literature. This reading has allowed us to pose some specific questions, as well as to keep other areas in mind. As we go through the evidence, however, we find our interpretation changing, as research questions prove too unrefined and new areas of interest arise. This has caused data-driven modifications of our original theory-driven research programme.

A crucial component of historical studies is the way in which pieces of evidence are addressed. In other words, what is accepted as a close approximation of past reality? Documents and other pieces of evidence originated not so that historians might know what really happened, but for other contemporary purposes. Sometimes the authors of documents faced constraints in the knowledge they had or the time available to check their sources. People make mistakes; they can also exaggerate or misrepresent. Newspapers − often an important source for historical context − are far from error free; even today they privilege speed of communication over accuracy of content. Newspapers can also exhibit very blatant political or social biases.

This search for biases, subtexts and mistakes lies at the core of historical enquiry.[34] It is here that the discipline of history makes its second great contribution. Historians are trained repeatedly in the evaluation of evidence. They seek likely biases in the authors or forms of evidence, and then look to internal consistency or external verification with other sources. This process must apply to both qualitative and quantitative evidence. Some researchers tend to accept quantifiable data (such as student record cards) at face value, arguing that no reason exists for bias − a naive, if convenient, rationalization. In the Beal case, the possibility exists that students tended to report a more 'respectable' parental occupation or a more successful placement. Outright errors are also possible. The use of outside sources can point out some of these things. Of course, some researchers would argue that an expressed occupation, by revealing personal class identification, tells us more about an individual than an actual occupation would.

Historians must treat other forms of evidence in the same way. In the case of oral testimony, memories can be coloured by later experiences, or can be simply mistaken. Even photographs must be interrogated. Are they posed or candid shots? Did the photographer choose a particularly photogenic background? Are we sure about the purported date or subject of the photograph? Researchers cannot simply dismiss oral and photographic evidence; they provide windows into areas that would otherwise be cast in darkness.

Having proceeded this far, one final screening of the evidence occurs, involving the historian's own subjective understanding of the past. If evidence fits the researcher's mental reconstruction of a particular lived reality, and if no reason exists to doubt the evidence on *prima facie* grounds, the evidence is accepted as a likely approximation of reality. If, however, evidence and understanding conflict, the historian must re-examine each. Since different researchers have different understandings of reality, this leaves the door open to disagreement, controversy and the sort of debate that can keep a discipline invigorated.[35]

History of education grew up at a time when history itself was highly constitutional and institutional in focus, when 'acts and facts' were widely supported. Moreover, in the educational domain itself it was a time when the organization, administration and alteration of educational structures and systems seemed at the heart of attempts to improve schooling. A move towards curriculum history assumes that we now take a different view: that analysis of organizational structure must be linked to a broader analysis of the legacies of status and resources, of curriculum and examination policy, if schooling is to be analysed and improved. To a point this is merely to echo the obvious – history of education like any subject has reflected our perceptions of the educational enterprise. At the present time we need a historical study of education which responds to our new perceptions of the sheer complexity of that enterprise.

The time has come for researchers to step into the schoolhouse of the past. The sources are there to make the trip worthwhile to the historian. The meanings, subtleties, contradictions and nuances are there to make it valuable for the curriculum scholar.

5 Vocational Education and School Reform: The Case of the London (Canada) Technical School, 1900–1930

IVOR F. GOODSON WITH IAN R. DOWBIGGIN

Between 1880 and 1930 educators in the United States and Canada pursued reform of the secondary school curriculum by introducing technical subjects such as industrial education, commercial studies and domestic science. In response to the growing popular demand for access to secondary schooling, and the perception that public education should be more relevant to the occupational needs of all children, educational officials and administrators committed themselves to a systematic differentiation of the high school curriculum into programmes of study designated as either 'practical' or 'liberal/academic'. However, what began in some instances as a sincere campaign to provide useful schooling for adolescents whose skills were more mechanical than academic emerged as a specific type of schooling which often reinforced gender, ethnic and socio-economic inequalities.[1]

Case studies of the differentiated curriculum promise to shed light on the social and political context of technical schooling and indicate new approaches to the history of education. Our examination of the origins of state technical education in London (Canada) suggests that, while a measure of consensus was reached among educators, businessmen and labour leaders at the provincial and national levels, curricular change was a hotly debated issue at the local level, often leading to conflict over the distribution of resources and funding among interest groups inside and outside the educational bureaucracy.

The struggle to develop and promote the London Technical School, one of the first of its kind in the Canadian province of Ontario, coincided with a sophisticated campaign that opposed the expansion of resources and facilities for technical education beyond the original provisions. Our research provides evidence that elements within the city's social and commercial elite made significant efforts to obstruct the progress of technical education at a time when it appeared that vocational forms of schooling might disturb the status of traditional, academic secondary schooling.[2] While state educators struggled to introduce technical schooling as another form of secondary public education with the resources, accreditation and physical plant to match, groups in local municipalities fought back in order to preserve the symbolic, cultural value of traditional academic schooling. The outcome, by the time of the Depression, was a messy compromise that was ultimately determined more by the ebb of federal and provincial funding for technical education in the 1930s than by the efforts of both public opponents and supporters of vocational schooling. None the less, the conflict over curricular change in London from 1900 to roughly the Second World War is historiographically significant because it shows that just as United States vocational reformers sometimes met resistance,[3] so reformers in London had to campaign aggressively to establish vocational education as a *bona fide* curricular option in that city's secondary schools.

This conclusion is based on ongoing research that, because of space limitations, does not address in the depth that they deserve issues like gender, labour history and schooling credentialism, factors that undeniably played crucial roles in the early years of the vocational movement. Still, we feel that the questions it raises point to the need for more studies which examine the deep structures of curricular differentiation and its ties to enduring patterns of social relations.

I

Secondary school vocationalism emerged in the province of Ontario in the first three decades of the twentieth century, part of a movement which swept through Canadian and United States schools and sought to smooth the transition between schooling and work for the many adolescents expected to enter secondary education after the turn of the century. Initially, much of the impetus of the technical education movement was due to innovative educators who, inspired by the ideas of Froebel and Pestalozzi, argued that schooling was most effective when all students were able to use their hands to complement the mental activity of learning. However, by the first decade of the twentieth century, the philosophy of 'social efficiency' had largely eclipsed this form of technical education. 'Social efficiency' reformers believed that the traditional high school curriculum, with its heavy emphasis on classical and academic subjects, was not suited to the interests, aptitudes and occupational needs of most students. They claimed that while the academic or 'humanist' curriculum prepared future teachers, lawyers, doctors and clerics for their adult jobs, it fulfilled no vocational purpose for the majority of young people who would later become industrial labourers, office workers or homemakers.[4]

'Social efficiency' in Ontario schooling derived its importance from the industrial, commercial, economic and social changes occurring throughout the province in the late nineteenth century. As manufacturing expanded dramatically and the surge of capital into the province became increasingly concentrated in a few hands and locations, the social landscape of Ontario was radically

transformed. Population growth and urbanization led to severe social disloca-
tion for many as industrialization broke down traditional rhythms of labour and
forms of production, including the apprenticeship system. Specialization,
mechanization and standardization increasingly dominated the work routine
on the shop floor.

Similar changes were occurring in commercial work. The expansion and
reorganization of manufacturing firms and financial corporations led to a rise in
the demand for office employees. Here, too, specialization and differentiation
of tasks predominated and coincided with the emergence of a new variety of
office worker, one who tended to be female and young, and was expected to
perform a strictly limited number of jobs.[5]

These changes in the nature of production and labour provoked a wave of
bitter strikes throughout southern Ontario in the years around the turn of the
twentieth century.[6] It was clear from the testimony given in 1888 to the Royal
Commission on the Relations of Labour and Capital that the introduction of
technical education was partially viewed as a way of reducing antagonism
between management and trade and craft unions.[7] Thus, it is hardly surprising
that the first and most vocal groups in favour of technical education in the
province were manufacturers' associations and boards of trade. The reasons
manufacturers and businessmen cited for the provision of technical education
varied. Yet there is no denying that groups such as the Toronto Board of Trade
and the Canadian Manufacturers' Association (CMA), an organization largely
centred in southern Ontario, ardently hoped that technical classes would neu-
tralize working-class discontent and end labour strife.[8]

The events that led to Ontario's Industrial Education Act of 1911 and the
federal government's Technical Education Act of 1919 constitute a history that
has been told by other historians. For brevity's sake, the campaign to introduce
technical education can be viewed as the result of a compromise among essentially three amorphous interest groups. The CMA, representing capital, was
impressed with the potential of technical schooling to improve the productive
skills of, and impose a form of institutional discipline on, the children of the
working class. Yet it was also fearful that this type of schooling might reduce
the distances between the social classes by expanding the opportunities of the
working classes for socio-economic mobility. Like their counterparts in
Europe, the wealthy and the industrial and commercial bourgeoisie of Canada
were willing to accept secondary schooling for the masses as long as it sharply
distinguished between 'liberal' and practical styles of schooling.[9] This, they
hoped, would have the effect of perpetuating and legitimating the social differences among classes through schooling, that is, exploiting the capacity of
educational systems to invest social distinctions with 'cultural meanings'.[10]

Reformers in the educational bureaucracy also supported the cause of technical education. Influenced by United States versions of 'social efficiency'
theory, they urged much larger enrolments in public secondary schools, often
for disciplinary reasons similar to those cited by the CMA. Yet their agenda
differed from the CMA's, as we shall see in our account of events in London.
Educational reformers sought to reduce the status distinctions between voca-

tional and academic schooling because they correctly perceived their career opportunities and material self-interests to hinge on this status divide. Educational groups tended to view vocationalism as a new career opportunity and one with the promise of enhancement in personal and professional terms. To achieve these goals they sought parity with established academic schooling. Their efforts to achieve this parity led to conflict in London between 1912 and the late 1920s.[11]

Organized labour, represented by the Trades and Labour Council (TLC), also supported the campaign for technical education and, like the educational bureaucrats, favoured a curriculum that featured a balance between technical and academic subjects. Organized labour was extremely suspicious of CMA intentions regarding the introduction of technical schools, but as long as these schools did not become simple 'trade schools' and were placed under public rather than private management, then it generally supported the cause.[12]

The compromise among these three groups, the CMA, the educators and the TLC, smoothed the way for the Industrial Education Act, passed by the Ontario provincial legislature in 1911. In brief, the Act authorized municipalities to establish a form of amplified schooling which complemented the already existing programmes in manual training and domestic science at the elementary and secondary levels and commercial education in certain high schools. The most important feature of the Act was that it promised provincial funding for industrial education, enabling municipalities across the province to offer technical classes for adolescents beyond the school-leaving age of fourteen.[13]

II

The new Industrial Education Act was good news to those in London who favoured technical education. London in the early twentieth century was a vibrant industrial and commercial centre with a reputation for conflict between labour and capital. Predominantly British in origin and Protestant in religion, its population numbered 50,660 in 1921, having almost doubled since 1881. Yet, as Bryan Palmer has shown, the Protestantism of London's working class was highly tinged by traditions of dissent and non-conformity that fed a popular culture of self-help and solidarity. The restlessness and independence of London's labourers did not go unnoticed by the editors of the *London Free Press*, the Conservative Party newspaper and mouthpiece for the city's white, male, Anglo-Saxon social elite. 'The inability of labour and capital to agree upon terms', it stated in 1901, 'is operating as the most serious check upon business which the country has to face.'[14] This was a compelling message for the city's industrial and commercial leaders who, in the years leading up to the First World War – years which witnessed the most rapid growth in the Canadian economy since the 1857–67 era – were committed to sustaining capitalist prosperity if nothing else. These were crucial years in another respect: the first two decades of the new century were also characterized by an influx of capital – often United States capital – and by the consolidation of business enterprises in Southern Ontario, and workers increasingly found themselves toiling in large factories. London was no exception. In the 1890–1920 period it swiftly said goodbye to its past of small-scale, artisanal industrial establishments and entered a new era of modern manufacturing and finance. Between 1901 and 1911, for example, the number of persons employed in London manufacturing rose from 5,675 to 9,413. The city boasted cigar-making, stove work, brass work, and biscuit and sweet factories that were among the biggest in the country. Then, in the 1920s, London's commercial and financial sectors blossomed. Between 1921 and 1931 Londoners employed in financial enterprises – which included the insurance, banking, investment and loan industries – rose in number from 820 to 1,448. This increase in financial occupations translated into the growth of clerical jobs for women: from 1921 to 1931, the number of women employed in clerical positions rose from 1,375 to 1,986.[15]

It is little wonder, then, that technical education was a topical issue in pre-First World War London. Following the national example, the first groups to put pressure on the London Board of Education were the London Board of Trade and an employers' organization called the Builders' Exchange.[16] The local chapter of the TLC was somewhat less enthusiastic, stressing that technical education ought to be much more than simple trade training, but it too welcomed efforts to found a new technical school in the city.[17] In particular, its newspaper, the *Industrial Banner*, applauded the introduction of night classes in industrial education and domestic science and advised 'every young man and woman wage-earner in London' to attend 'this their Workmen's University'.[18]

Some London educators also endorsed the idea of technical education. One was Herbert Benson Beal (1876–1956), a public school principal. A native Londoner, Beal had attended the course at Columbia University's Teachers College on industrial education in the first decade of the new century and was convinced that schooling ought to comply with the principles of 'social efficiency'.[19] Yet official support for technical education in London was also based on a specific and practical local consideration. Since the 1880s city educators and Board of Education trustees had suggested that provisions for technical classes would reduce the 'over-crowding' at the London Collegiate Institute (LCI), the city's only public high school. As the *London Free Press* editorialized on 7 November 1912, 'everyone' in London knew 'that a considerable percentage of students' attended LCI for only a year or two just 'to fill in time, getting very little benefit'.[20] It was widely thought that these students were better suited to a curriculum which taught them mechanical or commercial skills. A technical school would house these students, the thinking went, relieving congestion at LCI and saving the city the cost of erecting another academic high school. A further advantage of this plan for those in London who favoured collegiate schooling was that by removing from the collegiate institute the pupils whose occupational aptitudes appeared to be more industrial and manual in nature, a technical school would physically segregate working-class children and the sons and daughters of wealthy families during the secondary schooling years.

Despite the practical attraction of this proposal, on two occasions during 1911 the London Board of Education voted against taking the appropriate action to introduce technical education, a sign that not everyone thought highly of vocational schooling. As a member of the Board of Education had told the Royal Commission on Industrial Training and Technical Education on 18 October 1910, 'the older members of the board [of education], and the so-called City Fathers' on the City Council harboured a 'hide-bound antipathy against' educational reform, including the addition of technical subjects to the curriculum.[21] This 'antipathy' to educational reform on the part of the City Council may have derived to a great extent from the social class background of its members; as Armstrong has written, in the first three decades of the twentieth century 'The City Council [in London] tended to be dominated by the same type of conservative business leaders as in the past.'[22] However, the persistence of reformist employers such as E. R. Dennis and W. W. Gammage paid off. On 7 November 1911 their motion in favour of the establishment of night classes in industrial and domestic education was carried at the Board of Education with the understanding that the government would pay 25 per cent of the equipment costs and 50 per cent of the teachers' salaries. An Advisory Industrial Committee (AIC) was also established, a municipal body consisting of four elected and four appointed members authorized by the 1911 Act to oversee the development of industrial education. In January 1912 night classes began and in September a day school opened as well. Classes for both the day and night schools were held in two of the city's public schools. H. B. Beal was appointed principal of the new school, officially named the London Industrial and Art School.

The curriculum of the day school in its first few years was evenly balanced between practical and academic subjects. In compliance with the wishes of vocational reformers and organized labour, and in conformity with the ideas of educators like John Seath, whose 1911 report *Education for Industrial Purposes* formed the basis for the 1911 Act,[23] the new industrial school was not intended to be 'a trade school in the restricted sense of the term'.[24] Parents who sent their children to the school to be enrolled in either the boys' or girls' two-year terminal course agreed with officials like Beal that their offspring ought to receive both a practical education and a sound academic schooling.

Thus, the London Industrial and Art School became a reality because a coalition had formed by the second decade of the twentieth century in favour of the introduction of technical classes. This coalition was strong enough to overcome the reluctance of some members of the Board of Education and City Council to approve the founding of an industrial school, yet it also rested on a shaky foundation. Many educators, politicians and lay men and women were willing to give rhetorical and initial financial support when provincial funding was made available, but many also remained unconvinced that technical education deserved either the resources or the status that its most fervent advocates believed were crucial to its progress. The success of technical education in London hinged on its capacity to prove to these sceptics that a technical school would reduce student congestion at LCI and save the city the cost of building another collegiate. When in the upcoming years the technical school showed signs of costing much more money and of failing to solve LCI overcrowding, conflict was virtually guaranteed to break out.

III

The potential for conflict over technical education grew soon after the opening of the technical school in temporary accommodations in 1912. Francis Walter Merchant, Ontario's Director of Technical Education and a former principal of LCI, began to apply pressure to the London Board of Education between 1914 and 1916 to improve dramatically the facilities for day classes in technical education. The result was that in early 1916 the City Council approved the funds for erecting a new school building for technical purposes. However, the opposition Merchant encountered and the controversy over additional building and equipment costs that broke out several months later showed that many Londoners were unconvinced that the patently inadequate accommodations for technical classes needed to be improved.

Merchant believed that for technical education to be 'efficient' in Ontario, he had to overcome the reluctance of local municipalities 'to accept the responsibility for a radical change in policy and to provide the necessary school accommodation for the increased attendance' at day classes.[25] The problem was that municipalities were inclined to pay for only night classes or day schools like the London Industrial and Art School, which were housed in existing buildings and used existing equipment.[26] Despite the complaints of Beal and the AIC in 1913 that the poor classroom facilities for day school students did not meet the standards of the provincial Department of Education,[27] the city and Board of Education moved slowly towards solving the technical school's problems. It was plain, then, that while Londoners were willing to finance the construction of more public schools and additions to LCI, there were also many who were willing to ask the question, in the words of the *London Advertiser*, 'Why spend so much money on technical education in London?'[28]

Seeing London's hesitation in improving the facilities for technical education, Merchant made two trips to the city in January 1914 to convince Londoners that they ought to upgrade the quality of technical education they were offering. Merchant alleged that the accommodations, limited for the most part to the basement of one school and the rooms of another old and soon-to-be condemned school, were completely inadequate and were particularly unacceptable for the academic classes. 'Your main handicap in industrial education', he told Londoners, 'is lack of room. You give your work a black eye, to begin with, by putting your academic classes in a building not fit for public school purposes.'[29]

Merchant's appeals had little immediate effect. As he himself noted, with the outbreak of the First World War in the summer of 1914 most Boards of Education in the province were not inclined to sustain the financial burden of erecting new schools, especially for technical education.[30] Therefore, in 1915 Merchant resorted to new tactics. On 5 March Merchant informed the London Board of Education that the government grant of $9,500 for technical education was jeopardized 'unless assurances could be given that steps will be taken in the future to provide more suitable accommodations'.[31] Faced with the prospect of having either to pay all the costs for technical classes or to discontinue technical education entirely, the Board of Education was able to convince the City Council to authorize $35,000 for the purchase of a new site. This would not be the last time Merchant, representing the provincial Ministry of Education and its commitment to the expansion of state secondary schooling for the masses, would have to intervene in London to overcome resistance to the growth of technical education. In the meantime, having made these concessions, the City Council was determined to monitor closely the Board of Education's future spending plans with regard to technical education. Sensing potential friction, the Chairman of the Board at its 6 January 1916 meeting proposed that, if it got the approval of the Department of Education, the Board would recommend to the City Council the erection of a technical school building as a substitute for an East End collegiate institute. The Department approved the plan on 18 January and on 21 February the City Council granted the request of $165,000 for the construction of a technical school.[32]

This compromise between the Board of Education and the City Council may have resulted in approval for a new technical school building, but its terms indicated that technical education promoters in London had gained a highly qualified victory. The new technical school's future now rested more firmly than ever on its capacity to relieve the student crowding at LCI by attracting those pupils who supposedly wasted everyone's time by attending. In other words, the technical school was viewed as the institutional alternative for children whose educational interests were believed to be served by a curriculum oriented towards industrial, commercial and domestic skills. Its main purpose in the eyes of many of London's social and political leaders was to siphon off these students from LCI, thus making the collegiate a school for the academically able sons and daughters of the city's prosperous classes.

The social-class-oriented nature of the technical school was reinforced when it was suggested that it serve as a substitute for an East End collegiate institute. London's East End was the predominantly working-class part of town. An East End collegiate institute would, in the words of E. R. Dennis, 'encourage more children to attend [high school classes], particularly the sons and daughters of the working-men' of London.[33] The erection of a technical school rather than an East End collegiate institute was a convenient way of denying the city's working class access to academic secondary schooling, something for which East End community groups had been campaigning since before the First World War. It also ensured that the type of postprimary schooling most working-class adolescents received would be of a technical nature, and hence of lower status.

Technical education promoters barely had time to celebrate before a controversy erupted in the summer of 1916 over the Board of Education's spending plans for the new technical school. The public debate was largely generated by the *London Free Press*. In collaboration with the City Council, the *Free Press* attacked the Board for its plans to build a swimming pool, gymnasium and theatre for the school and to spend $9,500 beyond the original $165,000 to equip the classrooms. The *Free Press* and the City Council accused the Board of financial profligacy on the grounds that the new technical school was not an ordinary school. In the words of one controller on the City Council, 'I believe in an industrial school, but I do not believe in spending too much on it.'[34]

The *Free Press* claimed that its campaign against the building plans for the technical school was based solely on concerns for 'efficiency' in municipal administration and 'the interests of the taxpayers' of London,[35] but this was highly dubious, for it ignored the fact that the decision to recommend the construction of a technical school was, in the words of the chairman of the AIC, 'the most economic solution of two very pressing educational problems'. As chairman A. A. Langford explained in his address to the Board of Education on 27 June 1916, the city stood to save more by building a technical school for two important reasons: the provincial grant of $9,500 for the industrial school was substantially greater than that for a collegiate institute ($2,246); and the Department of Education paid for half the cost of salaries for technical instructors while contributing nothing towards the salaries of collegiate institute teachers.[36] However, the *Free Press*, unlike its competitor, the Liberal *London Advertiser*, chose to disregard most of Langford's argument. By so doing, it demonstrated that it was intent on judging the technical school according to different standards from those it applied to the financing and construction of a regular secondary school. In other words, it was reluctant to recognize the technical school and its form of schooling as equal in status to the city's collegiate institute.

The *Free Press*'s attitude to technical education during the spending controversy of 1916 was fairly typical of the way some Londoners viewed its value to the city and province. As the *Free Press* commented in 1916, 'The value of industrial education is a matter that is not disputed in any enlightened community', yet many who sat on the City Council were resolved that, if they could not prevent the construction of a new technical school, they would at least ensure that technical education continued to be low status and restricted to the 'less able' adolescents of the lower strata of society. The settlement of 1916 was possible only because some City Councillors felt confident that a new technical school would not seriously change these circumstances; indeed, its presence, some hoped, might actually accelerate the status differentiation and stratification of secondary schooling in London. As long as this perception prevailed, the 1916 settlement was viable. However, when technical education promoters like Beal and the members of the AIC began taking steps to improve the status of technical schooling after 1916, controversy again disturbed the early history of the London technical school.

IV

In autumn 1918 the new technical school building began to admit day students and in January 1919 it opened officially amid extensive press coverage and public attention. Yet despite the hoopla over the new school, unofficial attitudes to technical education were far from warm. For example, on 23 August

1918, the *London Advertiser* asked rhetorically, 'Did someone say something disparaging about the academic work of a technical school?' and noted the

> objection [that] has been made to technical education that it is not cultural; that it tends to develop along a certain line, and narrow the interests to a groove before a sufficiently broad knowledge of the things contained in books is acquired to supply a foundation on which to build up life work. Protest has been carried to the point of assertion that technical education has a tendency to develop 'efficient machines' instead of intelligent men and women.[37]

The persistence of doubts like these were a bad omen for those pursuing a broad liberal model of education through the technical school.

In autumn 1919 the school experienced its first full-fledged crisis. The measure that educators and politicians in London had hoped to postpone for the foreseeable future through the 1916 settlement – the erection of another collegiate institute – again seemed necessary by late 1919. Expedients such as the transfer of LCI's commercial classes from the commercial building on the site to the old Princess Avenue public school had not solved the overcrowding at the collegiate. Matters appeared to come to a head when the Board of Education submitted its building plans for 1920 to the City Council and was twice refused. The failure of the Board to obtain expenditures from the City Council for the erection of an East End collegiate institute in particular drew attention to the new technical school and its low enrolment. With the apparent failure of the technical school to alleviate the problem it had been built to address, proposals began to surface in autumn 1919 to use the technical school building for collegiate institute purposes.[38]

The eagerness to exploit the virtually brand new technical school building stemmed from another factor, however. Between 1916 and 1919 Beal and the AIC had declared their intention to improve the status of technical education by attracting not just the non-academic students who preferred to attend LCI, but also the academically able pupils who graduated from London's public schools. In his own words, Beal wanted to break 'the educational habit in Ontario, impressed by many succeeding generations, for children to go to the Collegiate Institute when they graduate from the Public School'.[39] As he had maintained as early as 1912,

> Vocational schools will appeal to and arouse many who our academic schools have failed to arouse. They have opened up a successful future for many a boy and girl who, by academic standards, would be accounted failures . . . But [they] are equally for those who have been successful in their academic studies. The prizes in the Industrial World for the efficiently trained are such as to claim our best.[40]

In a series of unpublished reports to the London AIC in 1917–18 Beal recommended launching 'an aggressive campaign to bring the school to the attention of those who should patronise it', a campaign which would undermine 'the popular impression shared by teachers as well as parents that boys and girls who show proficiency in school studies are necessarily adapted for and should be directed towards the learned professions'. Beal deplored the attitude shared by some 'educationists' that 'Vocational Schools are the natural dumping ground for all backward and defective children of other educational institutions', the 'class of more or less unfortunate pupils who are below the average mentally'. Too often, he contended, it was assumed that those who showed little talent for 'abstract thinking' were assumed to have 'native mechanical aptitude' and were despatched to a technical school. Beal's goal, one that was 'indispensable to the success of our Technical School', was to 'place [the Technical School] on an equality with other schools in the estimation of the public', and to accomplish this, he hoped to attract some of the academically able students of LCI.[41]

In other words, Beal sought to raise the status of technical education in London to the point where its credentials would be considered equal to those of LCI by convincing academically proficient students to enrol at the new technical school. Beal wanted to make the technical school a true 'common school' for high school age adolescents; like the Chicago opponents of the Cooley Bill in 1913, 1915 and 1917,[42] Beal realized that a stigma would continue to surround technical education as long as it was perceived to be distinct from the rest of the public school system. The spectre of Beal actually achieving this objective must have been daunting indeed to those families in London whose children attended LCI. They recognized that a secondary school system which sharply distinguished technical education from academic education also upheld the socially exclusive nature of LCI credentials. However, by the end of the First World War, it appeared that Beal and his allies were making progress in their attempt to eliminate the material and symbolic disparities between the two forms of secondary schooling. Technical education already enjoyed substantial financial support from the provincial government and in 1918 was awarded a brand new, well-equipped, state-of-the-art school building. In July 1919 the federal Technical Education Act received royal assent and signalled a decade-long investment of ten million dollars in technical education across the country, a measure which particularly benefited the technical schools in rich provinces like Ontario.[43] By contrast, LCI's building was far from new, having been erected in 1878. It also suffered from severe overcrowding in 1919, which a succession of provincial high school inspectors had warned would jeopardize the Department of Education's annual grant to LCI or force the province to close the school down.[44] With the situation unimproved by 1919, the contrast between conditions at the technical school and LCI led to acute resentment of technical education's material assets, a sentiment that persisted over the next six years as the conflict over money and resources for public schooling in London grew fiercer.

In autumn 1919, then, the *Free Press* spearheaded an attack which, at least in the eyes of the technical school's defenders, threatened its existence. In late September the *Free Press* publicized the misgivings expressed by C. R. Somerville, London's Mayor and a member of one of the city's most affluent families.[45] Somerville alleged that the technical school was cost-ineffective because the city paid on average over $300 per year to support each student in technical classes. With an enrolment of only 124 day students, the technical school was not easing overcrowding at LCI and the Mayor argued that it was ridiculous to maintain 'such a large building for the accommodation of such a small number of students', in the words of the *Free Press*. In a thinly veiled reference to the new technical school, the *Free Press* agreed with the Mayor's opinion that London school buildings featured 'Too many frills and not enough utilitarian thought' and along with the Mayor urged that part or all of the technical school be used for collegiate institute classes.[46]

In the midst of this imbroglio another problem surfaced to exacerbate the technical school's troubles. Beal and the AIC had been expecting the Department to confer official high school status on the technical school in autumn 1919, a gesture that would have enabled the school to offer matriculation courses for students who wished to attend post-secondary faculties of engineering and domestic science, and hence improve its chances of enrolling students who might otherwise attend LCI. Yet the Department of Education hesitated to approve the measure because the new headmaster, who served under principal Beal, supposedly did not have the proper qualifications for his position. The Department's delay provoked a heated response from W. N. Manning, the AIC chairman. He complained to the Department that the delay jeopardized the Board of Education's recent effort 'to attract to our school some of those in the Collegiate Institute who would profit most by the Technical School Course'. More ominously, Manning stated, the Department's actions threatened to 'give aid to those who are opposing Technical Education in London'. To Manning the risks the Department was taking were high. Its 'action', he argued,

> has precipitated a crisis in the affairs of our [technical] school as the Board [of Education] has always had considerable criticism of its building programme and at the present time our Mayor is publicly advocating the use of the Technical School building for Academic High School work . . . I must frankly admit that the continuance of the school is seriously endangered at the present time and a continuance of hair splitting over regulations will tend to increase the likelihoods of the building being turned over to pure academic high school purposes and a discontinuance of any further attempt to provide Technical and Industrial Education in London.[47]

Manning's letter coaxed the Department on 7 October 1919 into approving the technical school's new headmaster and the school became the London Technical High School. Indeed, Manning's interpretation of the matter may in fact have been either wittingly or unwittingly alarmist. None the less, the crisis revealed that technical education faced some formidable opposition in London in the early twentieth century.

The conferral of high school status briefly eased the situation for the technical school in late 1919. However, the matrix of secondary schooling in London and throughout Ontario was about to change. In April 1920 LCI burned down, virtually guaranteeing that pressure to use the facilities at the technical school for academic classes would resume. The loss of the LCI building was particularly serious because on 1 January 1921 the 1919 Compulsory Attendance School Act, which extended the age of full-time school attendance from fourteen to sixteen, came into effect. In addition, the Board of Education and East End and London South community organizations were campaigning for the erection of two new collegiate institutes. The prospect for the City Council of paying for these new collegiate institutes to house the swelling numbers of high school pupils again triggered efforts to use the technical school's class space for purposes other than industrial education.

The public debate over the loss of LCI revealed that many Londoners were willing to support technical education only as long as it served as a mechanism for limiting access to academic secondary schooling. To the *Free Press*, the destruction of LCI suggested the need to reconsider the city's building programme. On 4 February 1920 Merchant had visited London and urged the city to build new collegiate institutes in London South and London East, but some trustees on the Board of Education favoured building a new central high school to serve the whole city.[48] After the fire, the *Free Press* publicly endorsed Mayor E. S. Little's support for the centralized plan, which called for one elitist collegiate institute 'that would be a junior university run on university lines'. Mrs A. T. Edwards, a trustee who also favoured the one collegiate institute plan, recommended adding one year to the elementary school. This, she claimed, would temporarily solve the problem of accommodating the large number of first-year LCI students who were without classrooms. But the main attraction of her plan was that it echoed the age-old solution to LCI's overcrowding: it provided an extra year of primary schooling for the 'large percentage of pupils entering their first-year work' at the collegiate who later left anyway 'for the purpose of trade learning', additional time to consider attending a form of alternative secondary schooling like the technical school. Her plan was based on the assumption that the crowding at LCI was solely owing to those students who were destined for manual labour; in other words, the working class. According to the *Free Press*, the 'new plan' would ensure that pupils would enter the Collegiate Institute only as they had a definite vision of their life's work. Those desiring a more technical education would, it is stated, naturally gravitate towards the Technical and Arts Institute.[49] Thus, the destruction of LCI provided the opportunity to restructure secondary schooling in London in such a way that only the exceptional academic students would enter a new and modern LCI. The rest would be encouraged to attend the technical school.

However, as some citizens astutely observed, the one-CI plan would reduce the physical accessibility of CI education in London. Many insisted that a central CI for the entire city would make it difficult for students to attend. The *Free Press* countered by asking rhetorically, 'Is it too much to ask that students of the Collegiate age should walk, wheel, motor or street car' to a central CI?[50] This attitude prompted the charge that supporters of the one-CI plan were trying to restrict secondary schooling to a select few. As one letter to the editor of the *Free Press* alleged on 4 May 1920, 'one of the uppermost questions in the minds of citizens at the present time' is 'Should the Board of Education provide one or more Collegiate Institutes for the city of London?' The correspondent contended that centralization would be highly unfair to children from the city's suburbs and thus serve 'the self-interests' of wealthy 'Uptown people'.[51]

Despite the opposition of the *Free Press*, the city opted to build three new CIs after Merchant visited London in early May. He reminded Londoners that the Adolescent School Act was to come into effect shortly, and one CI and a technical high school would not be able to house the expected increase in secondary enrolment. Yet this decision simply raised questions about the usefulness of the technical school. With the city compelled to build three new CIs over the next few years, and with day attendance at the technical school in 1920–1 still unimpressive, pressure to use the technical school's classrooms for academic purposes began to mount again in the early 1920s.

As some Londoners increasingly coveted the resources of the technical school, others publicly discredited the type of schooling it offered. Groups like London's Building Contractors complained that the technical school was a haven for the 'many boys now looking for soft snaps'. As one contractor told the *Free Press* in June 1921, 'The Technical School is practically useless as it is at present . . . The school is certainly not doing what it was expected to do nor is it the benefit to the community that many think it is.'[52]

These negative comments were reportedly echoed by the city's Truant Officer, George Weir. In a 2 June 1921 interview with the *Free Press*, Weir allegedly stated that while night classes were useful, the day school did not teach manual skills 'and for that reason renders no lasting benefit to the community'. He urged that the school be turned into a commercial high school or an East End CI.[53]

For the next three years the *Free Press* persisted in its effort to publish stories that might injure the reputation of the technical school and prompt its conversion into an academic school. In May 1922, for example, one trustee of the Board of Education drew headlines in the *Free Press* for his suggestion that a committee be appointed to report on the possibilities of the technical school being used as an East End high school. Like others before him, he was tempted to support the use of the technical school for academic classes because of the common belief that it had a small enrolment and did not teach its students practical skills which would benefit industrial productivity.[54] On 9 May Beal disputed these charges at a meeting of the Board of Education. In particular, he denied the *Free Press*'s allegation that the technical school had room for 70–150 more pupils. In fact, he pointed out, with the anticipated increases in attendance because of the Compulsory Attendance Act, 'the total accommodation of the school will not begin to accommodate the Technical High School and Commercial High School students' in autumn 1922. Yet the *Free Press* virtually ignored Beal's data and instead tried to convey the impression that the technical school was a drain on the taxpayers of London.[55]

Things got worse for Beal and the technical school in 1923 when the Board again approached the City Council for funds to start a major building programme to house the swelling ranks of secondary school students who attended classes in the new Central Collegiate Institute and the temporary quarters in various public schools in London South and London East. The Board's plans to increase secondary school accommodation were opposed by the City Council and the *Free Press*, which followed its long-standing policy of attacking any proposal calling for greater physical access to a collegiate institute education. On 4 January 1923 the *Free Press* urged that a second Board of Trustees be elected to oversee the established Board's handling of secondary educational matters, presumably because another body would be less prone to requesting big budgets. The *Free Press* also criticized the London AIC, citing 'objections [which] have been heard with regard to the method of placing Technical School affairs in the hands of a group of men, only half of whom are elected by the people'. Similarly, the *Free Press* accused the members of the AIC of poor attendance at its meetings, a fact, it alleged, which indicated a lack of public interest among the incumbent members. The Board for its part retaliated by proposing to go over the heads of the City Council and submit its school budget to a popular vote.[56]

The poor relations between the Board of Education and the City Council simmered until December 1923, when conflict broke out again. This time the *Free Press* threw its weight behind the idea of a probe into the 'efficiency' of the technical school. It published allegations of an unnamed critic who charged that pupils in the two-year plumbing course were taught 'only the barest elementals of the trade', while in the second year of the course they repeated 'almost exactly the work of the first'.[57] With the coming of the New Year, the *Free Press*'s attack on the technical school did not abate as it continued to run stories on what it described as 'rumours of a possible enquiry into the conditions at the Technical High School'. On 2 January it stated that

> The recent criticism of the [technical] school aroused considerable interest among ratepayers and especially in school board circles. It is one of the sole topics of discussion at the city hall and there appears to be little doubt but that those citizens who are behind the proposal will receive a great deal of support when the question is brought to the attention of the board.[58]

One week later it quoted one trustee as saying that the technical school was 'the city's greatest educational waste'. Repeating the stock allegation that the technical school did not provide effective skills training, the Reverend Roy Mess, a newly elected member of the Board of Education, also charged that 'a large percentage' of the school's students were 'too indolent to take straight Collegiate training. They find it easier to wrestle with a chisel than to get down to hard study of educational fundamentals.'[59]

This attack on the technical school prompted replies from Beal and Arthur D. Hone, the Headmaster of the Technical School. In an interview with the *Free Press*, Hone reminded his audience that, far from being cost-ineffective, the Technical School had saved the city the cost of building a new collegiate institute. He also pointed out that the Technical School was being used in early

1924 by between 600 and 700 students, 'who would be forced to take High School work, as practically all enrolled here are under sixteen years of age'. He conceded that the Technical School had its share of 'lazy students, but not more than other schools of similar enrolment'. Thus, the charge that Technical School pupils were seeking 'to evade harder work at the Collegiate' was without merit.[60]

Beal was equally indignant. He told the *Free Press* on 12 January that the attacks on the Technical School had caused a breakdown of teacher morale. On 18 January he met with the AIC and the Board of Education and strongly cautioned Board members to investigate complaints about the Technical School before going to the press. 'Public criticism', he contended, could do 'temporary harm' to the Technical School because it

> tends to keep students from the school. Parents will naturally avoid a school that is under suspicion and students who would profit by the courses that the school provides will be so forced into other lines for which they are less suited and thus they miss the benefits of the school – the opportunity of education comes to the individual but once in their life time.

Beal shrewdly saw that bad publicity discouraged pupils 'whose need is for the class of education given in the Technical School' from enrolling there, a result which 'further overtax[ed] the other secondary school accommodation in the City'.[61]

Beal and Hone were plainly trying to prove that the Technical School was relieving overcrowding in London secondary schools because they feared that the criticism of 1923–4 was the prelude to another attempt to turn the school over to academic classes. In January 1924 their fears that such plans were being considered were justified. East End community groups were highly impatient with the city's failure to begin the construction of a collegiate institute in their part of town. With an estimated school budget for 1924 of one million dollars for expenses and half a million dollars for capital expenditures, the likelihood was great that the idea of using the Technical School to house collegiate institute students from the East End would surface. Indeed, despite the fact that Technical School enrolment had increased from 196 in 1921 to 663 in 1923, many were convinced that it was largely empty and was ideal as an alternative to a new CI.[62]

In fact, in 1924 one plan aimed to turn the Technical School into a vocational/collegiate, a composite high school offering programmes in both technical and academic education. It was promoted by three members of the Board of Education, who assured the public that this reorganization of the Technical School would not mean the end of technical education in London. However, the promoters of the Technical School were not so sure. At a heated meeting of the London Board of Education on 28 January 1924, Beal pointed out that the Technical School had plenty of academic classes; adding only a couple more to turn the school into a vocational/collegiate would do little except threaten provincial grants for technical education in London.

J. W. Hussey, the labour representative on the AIC, also expressed his opinion that such a step would lead to the disappearance of technical education in the city.[63]

The fears of Beal and Hussey that the composite school plan would jeopardize the future of technical education in London did not deter the *Free Press* from backing the proposal at the height of the controversy.[64] With the spectre of the Technical School being 'placed on an equality with other schools in the estimation of the public', in Beal's words, and the likelihood that the city would have to build a collegiate institute essentially for 'the sons and daughters of the working-men', the redefinition of the Technical School as a vocational/ collegiate was a way of frustrating the educational ambitions of London's working class in two crucial respects: first, by undermining the campaign to improve the status of the technical school; second, by denying the working class a full-fledged collegiate institute in its part of town. The secondary school matrix in London was changing radically in the early 1920s. Londoners faced the prospect of paying out of their own pockets for a new collegiate in the East End and the emergence of the Technical School as an equal partner in the high school system. Both developments challenged the monopoly which LCI had enjoyed up to that point. Hence one of the strategies for undercutting these developments was to turn the Technical School into a composite school which would never be of equal status to the collegiate institutes. The opposition of the Technical School lobby shows that this solution was certainly not in the interests of those promoting a broader notion of the Technical School because, as Beal acknowledged, it would threaten legislative grants to technical classes.

But this time the *Free Press* and its allies faced opposition from interest groups other than vocational supporters. The United Mothers' Clubs were equally opposed to the composite school plan. They refused to endorse the use of the Technical School for collegiate purposes, citing the fact that the school was not located in the East End and that some East End adolescents would have been compelled to travel considerable distances to go to school. But East Enders opposed the plan principally because they wanted a full-fledged collegiate institute and not a composite high school.[65]

By early February 1924 the battle over the future use of the Technical School had reached a new crisis point. On 5 February the *Free Press* published a front page story with the headline 'City pays over $300 per student at the Technical School', a headline which, appearing at the height of the debate, was patently calculated to discredit Beal's efforts to prove the cost-effectiveness of the school.[66] On 7 February representatives from the London South and East Parents' Associations met the Board. Despite being told that the City Council 'held the bag', controlled 'the purse strings' and was not in favour of an East End collegiate institute, the East End deputation reasserted its wish for a institute in its part of town.[67] At the same time Board support for the conversion plan was dwindling. On 6 February the Board's special committee looking into the conversion scheme met Merchant in London. He told the committee that there would be no legislative grants for the academic portion of the proposed composite school and disclosed that the Department of Education would only approve the plan if the city added an auditorium, playground and gymnasium to the existing school. It was a moot point anyway, Merchant explained, because the Department normally did not approve composite schools for cities of over 25,000 people.[68]

Given all these factors, the committee advised the formulation of alternative solutions to the secondary school problems of the city.[69] A consensus was reached whereby M. M. Simms, the chief attendance officer, was named as a vocational guidance officer with the mandate to 'use all his influence as such to fill the Technical School to overflowing', beginning in autumn 1924. Vocational guidance, it was decided, rather than the conversion of the Technical School into a vocational/collegiate, would be the solution to the problem of convincing the 'great many young people' who were 'wasting their time' by attending academic classes at the city's collegiate institutes to enrol in the Technical School and receive 'more useful training'.[70] On that note, the crisis subsided and the Technical School was safe for the time being. Once again though, a settlement was only reached by accepting subordinating conditions. The objective remained the relief of collegiate institute 'overcrowding', but now vocational guidance was being promoted to steer the more indolent collegiate institute students towards the Technical School.

The crisis of 1923–4 for the most part ended any chance to convert the Technical School into a collegiate institute. The most likely reason was the school's success by the late 1920s in easing demand for secondary schooling at the three collegiate institutes. For example, between 1921 and 1926 full-time attendance at the Technical School jumped from 192 to 957. By the onset of the Depression the Technical School, besides drawing over 40 per cent of all students in the city with High School Entrance standing, was attracting more and more adolescents without these same credentials.[71] For example, in 1927, 20 per cent of all Technical School pupils did not have their High School Entrance qualifications and by 1931 this figure had risen to 45 per cent.[72] In other words, the Technical School was finally serving the purpose which many Londoners had hoped it would when the school had been built between 1916 and 1918. It was relieving overcrowding at the collegiate institutes and accommodating the academically less able pupils of the city compelled to attend school until the age of sixteen. London's secondary school system had developed into one that deferred to the principle of mass schooling while maintaining rigid curricular distinctions in terms of status and 'cultural capital'.[73] By the arrival of economic hard times in the 1930s, then, the Technical School had emerged as a fundamental part of the city's secondary school system and a contributor to the reproduction of a differentiated social structure.

V

What conclusions can be drawn from this examination of the origins of technical education in London? The most obvious is that vocational promoters encountered stiff opposition in the early years from constituencies such as the

City Council and the *London Free Press*, which tended to represent the interests of London's ruling elite. This group, although by no means homogeneous, was none the less disposed to support technical education only as long as it was low-status, cost very little and helped to relieve collegiate overcrowding. In other words, they supported technical schooling as long as it was recognized as the secondary school for those who, because of their social origins, were disqualified from attending the collegiate institute. The early history of vocational schooling in London, then, suggests the possibility that events there were not unique and may have been repeated in other municipalities in Ontario, Canada and the Western world.

As recent histories of the curriculum have shown, attempts to make practical forms of knowledge in public schooling equal in prestige to academic knowledge have encountered resistance that had little to do with the educational interests of most pupils. When vocational promoters like Beal sought to improve the status of technical knowledge by attracting more 'able' students, augmenting its resources and expanding its facilities, while at the same time teaching the traditional academic subjects from an industrial and commercial perspective, they threatened the interests of those in London who rightly saw that the status of practical knowledge was tied closely to the success of its promoters in competing for provincial funding. Thus, there seems to be some truth to Young's comment that 'movements to make the scope of knowledge in a curriculum less restricted (a decrease in specialization), and the relations between knowledge areas more "open"' will be perceived by ruling groups as threatening to 'the patterns of social relations'.[74] Technical education in London constituted such a threat to the academic curriculum of the collegiate institute and the reaction of the *Free Press* and the City Council showed that many influential Londoners were intent on confronting this challenge, albeit under the guise of a campaign dedicated to fiscal 'efficiency'. In retrospect, then, the opposition to technical education in London in the early twentieth century resembled the Tory High Church opposition to mass schooling in nineteenth-century Britain, described by Carl Kaestle.[75] Many Londoners appeared to share the Tory High Church suspicion that mass state schooling would disrupt the social structure by making members of the lower classes unfit for their future occupational roles. As some American conservatives argued, free secondary education posed an even greater threat to social stability, deference and discipline. The fear that mass secondary schooling would tempt young men and women to desert the working roles their birth had destined them to fill was expressed by the Kansas poet Walt Mason, whose syndicated column was published in the *London Free Press*: 'Still the schools go on cramming the young with knowledge few of them will ever need; spoiling excellent farmers to make third-rate lawyers; ruining promising plumbers to furnish some more spellbinders.'[76] Opposition to mass secondary schooling in London followed the European pattern identified by Margaret Archer; oppositional groups lobbied for a rigidly stratified system when it appeared that they would be unable to stem the tide in favour of mass state schooling at the high school level.[77] Some of the questions that await further historical research are: who

were these Londoners who tried to undermine the efforts of curricular reformers? Were their social origins similar to those of Europe's elites who also
distrusted the widening of access to secondary education?

The legacy of the technical education movement of Ontario was less its
success at breaching the high school curriculum than its mobilization of the
defenders of academic curricula who wished to ensure that this type of curricular organization remained high status and hegemonic. Indeed, as Robert Stamp
has argued, Ontario high school educators were remarkably successful in resist-
ing curricular reform movements, particularly from south of the border. For
example, 'social purposes' theories failed to penetrate the classroom, as university, department of education and school personnel rejected the 'life adjust-
ment' syndrome of the United States high school curriculum. For students in
academic or matriculation programmes – and that included the vast majority –
classroom life continued to be circumscribed by a prescribed curriculum of
traditional subjects, authorized textbooks, deductive teaching and external examinations.[78] The history of the struggle over the London Technical School
testifies to the enduring resilience of this curricular phenomenon and reinforces
the conclusion that curricular conflict has ties to the shifting patterns of social
relations underlying the origins of state schooling.

6 Subject Status and Curriculum Change: Local Commercial Education, 1920–1940

IVOR F. GOODSON WITH CHRISTOPHER J. ANSTEAD

The first four decades of the twentieth century saw substantial transformations in systems of secondary education throughout North America. Social, economic and legislative changes brought new clienteles and new courses to schools – both state and private – in all regions of the continent. In Ontario, for instance, total secondary school enrolment increased from 21,723 in 1900 to 119,652 in 1940, while the number of secondary schools rose from 131 to 489 – among the latter were fifty-nine vocational institutions, symbolizing the changing orientation of North American education.[1] These adjustments inevitably altered the professional status of teachers and educators associated with particular disciplines. In cases where their status declined, some subject teachers and administrators employed curriculum change as a way to increase the material or symbolic resources available to them.

A case study of commercial studies in London, Ontario, illustrates this intersection of curriculum change and subject status. During the middle of the 1920s two major changes transformed commercial studies at the London Technical and Commercial High School. This chapter argues that these curriculum changes represented a response to declining subject status. During the quarter century preceding these changes, commercial studies in London declined from its position as a high-status department in the prestigious Collegiate Institute, being first marginalized in that institution and then transferred to the technical school. These changes took place at a time when the subject's student clientele had become feminized and, with the transfer to the technical school, proletarianized. Commercial educators viewed the change in student characteristics as causing the decline in their subject's status (and thus in their own professional standing). They introduced two new courses in an attempt to change both the class and gender characteristics of commercial students. In the end, these initiatives led to an educational experience increasingly segregated and structured by class and gender characteristics.

The period of change in North American education from the 1890s to the 1930s has attracted a good deal of scholarly attention. A 'post-revisionist' interpretation[2] provides a framework for understanding curriculum change in London, Ontario – a city of roughly 70,000 people (in 1930) with an economy based on brewing, manufacturing and financial services. In particular, the works of Herbert Kliebard, Harvey Kantor and David Labaree have provided clear elucidations of the patterns of conflict between various social and ideological forces involved in the construction of early twentieth-century American education.[3] Kantor and Labaree have drawn attention to the semi-independent roles played by educators and students in the construction of curriculum; neither group acted simply as puppets of external interests.[4] Both studies are particularly relevant to the present investigation: Kantor's because it examines the vocational movement, including commercial education; Labaree's because it is firmly grounded within a case study of a particular school. In addition, Jane Gaskell and Nancy Jackson have produced a short study of commercial education in two Canadian provinces, which provides crucial background to our exploration.[5]

The concept of subject status used in this chapter emerges from a definition used by researchers dealing with the status of individuals; this definition sees status as deriving from ownership of and control of access to material and symbolic capital.[6] Subject status essentially represents the collective professional status of subject teachers.[7] Its material side may consist of remuneration in cases where teachers in different departments receive different salaries. It can also cover career prospects, which may increase, for instance, when a subject earns departmental status. The material capital of a subject also consists of the collective resources, in terms of buildings, classrooms and equipment, which determine the working conditions for subject teachers. The symbolic side of subject status includes the authority or respect accorded to the subject, as well as the extent to which it controls access to a form of knowledge deemed valuable. This knowledge can be described in terms of cultural capital or credentials; its value reflects the degree of desirability of the opportunities for future prospects opened to the subject's students.[8] This chapter further argues that, in the early twentieth century, a discipline's symbolic capital derived partly from the perceived value of the student body, and could change as a result of transformations in student socio-economic characteristics.

Commercial studies, which moved from the Collegiate Institute[9] to London's Technical High School in 1920, underwent a major curriculum revision in the middle of the decade; as a result, the commercial course evolved from a single common general course into three courses of different lengths, with different emphases, aimed at different groups of students. The discipline had already experienced one major change at the start of the decade, when the Provincial Department of Education ordered its extension from two to three years. According to Principal Herbert Benson Beal, this allowed students to train for 'the higher positions in mercantile life'.[10] At the same time, the school allowed students the choice of leaving after two years with a 'junior diploma', which Beal described as adequate preparation for 'junior and stenographic positions'.[11] At this point, though, all commercial students enrolled in the same general course. The first major exception to this rule took the form of a one-year Special Commercial course created in 1924. This course admitted only those students who already had several years of secondary school experience. It served to attract dozens of young women (and smaller numbers of young men) who had finished their academic education at one of London's prestigious academic schools – styled as Collegiate Institutes – or, in a few cases, other schools. Because these students had already obtained a grounding in academic subjects at their previous school, the special one-year course features only strictly vocational classes.[12]

In 1926 the school announced the formation of a 'special business course for boys', (which became a 'general business course for boys' in 1933).[13] This new course had a different focus from the general commercial course; while the older course trained students to take general office positions, the new course trained male students for positions at wholesale firms and financial institutions, or in sales. As Beal pointed out, the course would prepare young men to work in places where they could find 'ample opportunity for advancement'.[14]

Why did these changes come about? One obvious hypothesis, that the provincial government insisted on their introduction, does not fit the evidence. Certainly, in both cases the provincial department allowed or authorized these changes, but they did not demand them. It was a purely local decision to take advantage of these options, and one that Principal Beal seems primarily to have made. Neither the local Board of Education nor the Advisory Vocational Committee – which oversaw the school's operations – urged Beal in this direction; instead they simply reacted to his decisions.[15] On the other hand, a lack of documents makes the question of whether Beal felt some pressure from commercial teachers in the school unanswerable, though that seems a reasonable contention.

Why did Beal (probably acting in conjunction with commercial teachers in his school) decide to introduce these courses, and what interests did they serve? If the new courses were to serve the interests of the students, then they should have changed the school experience in some way. In fact, the two innovations did little to alter existing practices. The special commercial course did not change anything for students at the Technical School, since they could not take it. Instead of making improvements for an existing student clientele, the course sought to attract another group of students. Had this new group consisted of young people who would otherwise have left the educational system, the change would have represented a laudable attempt to build on the school's original mandate. The new course, however, did not seek out the otherwise unschooled, but instead aimed at attracting educated youths away from private business colleges or even from the Collegiates.

On the other hand, the creation of separate courses for males only marked the public confirmation of a pattern that had existed for years. From the first years of commercial courses at the Technical School, the classes had a slightly different curriculum for each gender. The new course promised an emphasis on penmanship, business correspondence, accountancy, investment maths and salesmanship; yet the male classes in the general commercial course already featured more of an emphasis on accountancy than did those for females. The existing separate classes in other subjects for each gender would have allowed for an emphasis on penmanship, business correspondence or investment mathematics if desired. The only real change in curriculum came with the introduction of a class in salesmanship; the introduction of a brand new course was primarily a feat of legerdemain.[16]

The existing gender differences in curriculum fit into a wider pattern in the school (and of course wider patterns beyond the school); although all Ontario schools were premised on the American model of coeducation, female students at the technical school followed a different curriculum from males.[17] Besides the obvious differences in the technical subjects taken by each gender, males at the school took algebra throughout their course, whether they had entered a general technical, matriculation or general commercial stream, while only those few females enrolled in the matriculation course took algebra, and they only took it from the second year. In the technical department, females took art but males did not.[18]

Since the two new courses in no way responded to student demands, they seem to have been created mainly for the educators themselves. Commercial teachers did have definite occupational concerns at the time. In particular, they faced a clear decrease in the status of commercial studies, which occurred during the period from the turn of the century to the 1920s.

During the late nineteenth century commercial studies managed to amass substantial symbolic and material resources in the Ontario school system. From mid-century, classes in such business subjects as bookkeeping and penmanship became standard in the province's secondary schools. As demand for this sort of professional training grew during the second half of the nineteenth century, private business colleges proliferated, emphasizing a purely practical curriculum and guaranteed placement for graduates. The Ministry of Education also responded to this demand, introducing a one-year commercial course in 1885, and extending it to two years in 1896.[19]

In London at this time, commercial subjects made up part of the general academic curriculum at the city's Collegiate Institute. Commercial studies commanded increasing authority, and in 1895 became a separate department, with a distinct course of study, at the Collegiate Institute. In 1899 the commercial department moved to a new four-room building adjacent to the older CI building. From that point on, reports of attendance at the school listed students in the commercial department separately.[20] Both these actions point to an acknowledgement of the amount of symbolic capital controlled by commercial education at the end of the nineteenth century; departmental status provided material resources in terms of additional teaching positions up to and including department head, while the new building represented a high standard of working conditions. Indeed, the incoming Chair of London's Board of Education confirmed this status in 1899 when he declared the primary role of the local system to be the provision of 'a good English and Business education'.[21]

The success of commercial studies in the late nineteenth century reflected the association of office work with middle-class male respectability. Middle-class men in the late nineteenth century viewed clerical work as the first, obligatory, rung on a ladder of commercial success. Young men who wanted to make up the next generation of merchants, bankers or entrepreneurs knew they had to serve their time as clerks, bookkeepers or secretaries. Many educators, worried about the movement of young women into the high schools, saw commercial courses as a way to make school more relevant and attractive to these male students.[22]

Although the achievement of departmental standing, and quarters in a new building, resulted from commercial studies' high status at LCI, the physical and administrative separation from academic subjects made the department much more vulnerable to marginalization as its cultural authority decreased during the opening decades of the twentieth century.[23] At this time the symbolic capital associated with the value of the subject dropped throughout North America; thus the 1900 annual report of Ontario's Minister of Education quoted the opinion of the President of Harvard University on commercial courses, which he saw as 'hopelessly inferior to other courses'.[24]

The physical resources which contributed to the status of commercial studies reflected the subject's large enrolment at the turn of the century; a province-wide decline in enrolment in the early twentieth century accelerated the decrease in subject status. In 1902, 11,334 students in Ontario secondary schools took bookkeeping among their subjects. By 1922, that number had fallen to 6,524. The increase in absolute enrolment made the relative decline in the attraction of commercial studies even greater. Almost half (46 per cent) of Ontario's secondary students took bookkeeping in 1902; twenty years later, the proportion had fallen to less than 15 per cent.[25]

In London, the decline in commercial education's status led to marginalization, beginning early in the new century with the establishment of domestic science classes in the commercial building, thus reducing the material resources controlled by commercial teachers. Domestic science classes were held in the commercial building from 1903, and by 1907 the commercial building had become too crowded.[26] In 1908 the 'severe overcrowding' had reached the point where one commercial class consisted of sixty-two pupils sharing eleven typewriters. Some of the pressure eased later that year with the transfer of domestic science classes to the basement of the main building.[27] The commercial building remained crowded as it aged, and teaching conditions worsened. In 1915 the principal reported an average class size of forty-nine, despite provincial regulations limiting class size to thirty. By that point, the principal was talking of 'separating the Commercial Department from the rest of the Collegiate work'.[28]

After the end of the war, overcrowding at the commercial building reached a crisis point. In 1918 the Board authorized the removal of a staircase so classes could be held in a hallway, and the creation of a new classroom in the attic.[29] Finally, in 1919 the Board decided to act. At first they considered a new building in a site distant from the CI since, in their opinion, 'it would be preferable to have the Commercial Classes entirely separated from the Collegiate Institute.'[30] When the City Council refused to allow the funds for this, the Board decided to move the commercial classes into an old, decrepit, elementary school building, used by the military during the war; academic classes would move into the former commercial building. Even these poor quarters did not provide immunity for the commercial department; in September 1919, academic classes which could not fit in the other two buildings took over one of the department's six classrooms.[31]

The transfer of the commercial department to the London Technical High School in the early 1920s represented another stage in the subject's downward trajectory. The Technical High School had a remarkably different status from the Collegiate Institute, a difference based in the symbolic, rather than the material, realm. One of the chief factors behind the formation of the London Industrial School (later the London Technical and Commercial High School) in 1912 was a desire to ease overcrowding at the Collegiate Institute by the transfer of students who only attended the school for a year or two, before entering the industrial workforce. Enthused by the claims of the movement for social efficiency, London educators undertook the implementation of a school which would prepare these students for their expected careers.[32]

Thus, from the start, the Technical School suffered under the image of an institution for less desirable students. The school's first principal, and prime mover in its creation, Herbert Benson Beal, did not take this complacently; instead he fought to raise the public's estimation of his school by attracting students who had achieved high school entrance standing. Beal wanted to challenge, and, in the end, destroy a widespread perception of technical schools as 'the natural dumping ground for all backward and defective children'.[33]

The willingness of both federal and provincial levels of government to fund technical schooling handsomely at this time provided an important boost to Beal's campaign, and brought control over considerable material resources to the school. The construction of a brand new building (completed in 1918) filled with up-to-date equipment, seemed to signal Beal's complete victory, and caused many traditionalists, led by the *London Free Press*, to attack the Technical School on a variety of issues, all underpinned by a feeling that this new form of schooling presented a serious challenge to the cultural dominance of traditional elite academic education.[34]

The last of the campaigns of opposition took place in 1923 and early 1924. This campaign started with a series of attacks by the newspaper and council members which maligned the school in terms of its standards of teaching. Opponents also described the school as an inefficient part of the local system, claiming that it was too expensive and too little used.[35] The climax of this campaign came with a movement to convert the Technical School into a comprehensive high school, combining academic and technical streams. While this would have prevented the resulting school from challenging the Collegiate Institute on status grounds, it also promised to eliminate another problem – the growing need for some kind of secondary school in the city's predominantly working class East End. The combined weight of technical education supporters, spokespeople for the East End community who wanted their own CI and provincial officials opposed to the comprehensive plan finally scuttled this movement.[36]

Despite victories like this, and the early burst of funding from provincial and federal sources, any increase in status experienced by the Technical High School proved short-lived. Neither of these factors led to any great increase in symbolic capital, since the key distinction between practical and academic forms of knowledge remained firmly in place. In 1926 the Board eliminated all the manual training and domestic science classes from the city's Collegiate Institutes (by that point the city had three), making the distinction between these schools and the technical school more sharp.[37]

Despite Beal's efforts, his school remained starved of symbolic capital. A teacher who arrived at the school in 1930 remembered how a 'general feeling' existed 'that you were rather an inferior type if you attended Beal Tech. It was for the people who just didn't have the ability or didn't belong to the right class of people.' Or, put another way, 'if you weren't very bright you went to Tech. And [you also went] if your family was poor.'[38]

In 1920, this technical institution, burdened with continuing status problems, became the new home of the commercial studies department formerly associated with the Collegiate Institute. The destruction by fire in April 1920 of the CI building only hastened the implementation of existing plans to move the commercial students to the Technical School. Within days of the disaster, administrators worked out a new arrangement; academic classes from the burned-out building moved into the classrooms occupied by commercial courses, and commercial courses moved to the Technical School building. Although the commercial department remained administratively connected to the Collegiate for several months, the move proved permanent; the commercial department became an official part of the Technical School a year after the fire and emergency move.[39] Commercial education, once a highly respected component of the LCI curriculum, had now been consigned (along with domestic science and industrial education) to the Technical School building.[40]

In 1924, facing this situation of declining status, commercial educators embarked on a set of curricular changes to increase the material and symbolic resources of their department. They had the full support of principal Beal, constantly concerned with his school's status, which had been seriously threatened in the previous eighteen months. One way to increase the material resources of the discipline was to increase enrolment, resulting in a greater number of paid positions available to teachers of the subject and a greater voice in the distribution of other material resources. The provincially ordered expansion to a three-year course in 1921 had certainly contributed in this vein, but such an increase in bodies seemed to have little effect on symbolic wealth. The reforms initiated at the middle of the decade, by contrast, aimed to increase material resources, with more students and more courses, but they also evinced a concern with symbolic resources, through the recruitment of new student clienteles. This underscores the beliefs of the educators involved that student characteristics had an effect on subject status.

Taking the second reform first, the creation of a gender-segregated course represented a reaction to the observation that commercial classes, like commercial work, had become dominated by females. A perception that this fact had negative status implications caused commercial educators throughout the continent to seek some means of redressing the balance. Many business teachers sought to model their subject on the increasingly prestigious professional schools, which laid a heavy emphasis on masculinity; the presence of a female student body seemed to threaten this goal.[41] Of course, such concerns were unique to neither commercial studies nor North America. For instance, Brian Doyle, examining English studies in the United Kingdom, concludes: 'during the inter-war period English was . . . securely established as a stable and male-dominated professional field despite the presence of a majority of female students.'[42] In London, these concerns led to the decision to offer a special course to attract more young men.[43]

In the twentieth century, the respectable and male aura of commercial studies started to diminish as more and more positions for women opened up in clerical work. The Canadian economy underwent great changes in the generation surrounding the turn of the century. A fairly sudden transformation from entrepreneurial to corporate forms of capitalism meant that the volume of clerical work increased, and offices became the central directing agencies of huge economic entities. In an effort to rationalize these new phenomena, and maintain power in the hands of managers, clerical tasks became specialized and routinized. The new positions did not call for a few generalists with a wealth of skills, but for various specialists with limited skills; thus they paid poorly and offered little chance of advancement. These jobs did not suit the aspirations of most males entering the business world, but they did seem a step above traditional female paid work as a domestic or factory worker; female clerical workers flooded into the Canadian office in the first thirty years of the twentieth century.[44] By 1931, women held almost half of all clerical jobs in the country; over half of these women worked as typists and stenographers. In these junior positions, women outnumbered men by a ratio of more than twenty to one.[45]

Commercial education itself changed in reaction to these transformations. The addition of new subjects like stenography and typewriting around the turn of the century showed a curriculum adaptation to new circumstances. The commercial student body also reflected this new reality; by the time commercial education was widely and successfully established in the province, the majority of students enrolled in such courses were probably female. Young women ignored the wishes of mainstream educational reformers, who proclaimed the merits of domestic science, and eagerly sought the training which prepared them for the flood of new clerical jobs.[46] In an unpublished study, Gail Posen has found that women outnumbered men by a ratio of three to one in Toronto's High School of Commerce, from 1911 through to the Second World War.[47] In 1930, the six strictly commercial high schools operating in the province all reported a similar dominance of female students, who made up over three-quarters of the 6,721 students enrolled at those institutions. These figures tie the Ontario experience to that of American schools, which also saw a female majority in commercial classes appearing in the first decades of the twentieth century.[48]

London was not immune to these provincial, national and international trends. Increasingly in the twentieth century, women took jobs in the city's clerical workforce. A comparison of the census figures for 1911 and 1921 provides a small illustration of this movement. In 1911, London's banks employed 121 male clerks and twenty female clerks, while its insurance offices employed fifty-three male and thirty-six female clerks. By 1921, the number of male bank clerks had increased by only one, and the number of male insurance clerks dropped by twenty-four; over the same period, the numbers of female bank and insurance clerks increased by eighty-one and eighty-two, respectively. Twenty years later, 2,393 women held commercial positions in London.[49]

At the same time that women became a fixture in London's offices, their younger sisters started to change the matrix of local secondary education. From the start of the new century, girls frequently outnumbered boys at the Collegiate. Many of them ignored the domestic subjects, introduced to the local curriculum in 1902.[50] Instead they chose to take commercial studies, leading to a female dominance in the subject. Commercial studies had certainly become feminized by the time the programme came to the Technical School in 1920. A list of commercial diplomas awarded by the school in the first year of commercial studies included twenty-eight female names and only six male names. In 1923 the group of students entering the first year of the commercial programme numbered seventy-one females and only nineteen males.[51] A similar ratio continued to mark the commercial programme through the next two decades. In 1930 the number of students enrolled in commercial classes included 462 young women and 105 young men. In 1940 the school awarded eighty-five intermediate certificates in commercial studies, of which seventy went to young women.[52]

The possibility that this female influx had major repercussions for subject status resides in the nature of gender roles and relations at the time. In education, as in so many areas of early twentieth-century life, the experience of London's women and girls differed markedly from that of the city's men and boys. A wealth of evidence supports this interpretation at the level of the Board of Education and, especially, at the level of the teaching staff; it must have held true at the level of student.

Women in London had little representation on their Board of Education, the locally elected body which supervised the city's shools. Although one female trustee did serve a single term at the end of the nineteenth century, women only started to achieve sustained representation on the Board from 1919. Although the 1920 Board included four women out of fourteen trustees, for the next few years the Board included only one or two women at a time. In 1928 the board reduced itself to six members. The number of women members stayed constant at one or two until at least 1940. Women trustees took another important step with the election of the first female Chair of the Board in 1929, followed by two more women in that office in 1933 and 1934.[53] Although the representation of women on the Board did increase over time, it never reached an equality with that of men in this period, despite the fact that both streams of feminism – maternal feminism and equal rights feminism – had an interest in education. One of these pioneer female trustees reflected the prevailing denigration of women's experience when she concluded her report of an annual convention to the Board by regretting that no male trustee from the city had attended the convention and adding: 'My report is only from a woman's viewpoint.'[54] The deadpan delivery of sixty-year-old minutes prevents us from listening for any trace of sarcasm.

Women teachers experienced vastly different professional lives from those of their male colleagues. As in other places, London's female teachers faced discrimination in terms of status, both through official decisions on things like salaries or promotions and in the general level of treatment they received. A definite and formal gender differentiation appeared in the salaries paid to teachers. As an example, the 1932 salary schedule for the London Board paid female elementary school teachers with a first class certificate a maximum of $1,800 a year, while those with a second class certificate could receive up to $1,600; the corresponding maximums for male teachers stood at $2,500 and $2,400 respectively. The terms for teachers in secondary schools were more equal, but a formal difference remained; thus teachers in the highest category received $3,400 a year if male and $3,200 if female.[55] Of course, this latter statistic had little meaning for the majority of women teachers, who were clustered at the elementary level.

In terms of promotion, women could not move above the level of classroom teacher. Technically the Board did allow female principals in schools containing fewer than eight rooms, but in practice this meant that one teacher in each of the schools (only two operated in 1928) that had only two full-time teachers received the title of principal, with little increase in pay or status.[56] In the secondary schools, women could not become a department head outside the female technical subjects.[57] Advertisements for job openings always sought candidates in terms of gender; the Board ignored any women who applied for a male job unless they could find no suitable man. One teacher recalled her experience of being hired during the Depression: 'they wanted a commercial specialist, they wanted a man; but apparently they couldn't get a man, so they took me.'[58]

Simply stated, school authorities treated female teachers as second-class employees. The Board expected women teachers who married to give up their positions, and would only consider hiring a married woman, even for a substitute position, in an emergency.[59] When a Chair of the Board of Education spoke in favour of introducing mandatory retirement, he saw no problem in suggesting that men retire at sixty-five and women at fifty-five years of age.[60] Of course, this all took place in a society that by and large took such things for granted. Many female teachers themselves felt that it was simply logical that men have higher pay, that only men became principals, and that women should drop out when married and turn their attention to raising a family.[61]

The creation of a special commercial course for boys in 1926, then, represented an attempt to alter the slide in subject status through the recruitment of a

Table 1   Percentage of students entering first year of any commercial course, by gender

	1923	1927	1931	1935
Male	21	20	21	24
Female	79	80	79	76
n	91	325	292	406

Source: LTCHS student record cards

more socially valued student clientele. Did it succeed? Did the introduction of the course actually change the gender split in the subject? The answer has to be negative. Table 1 outlines the gender division in new commercial students, taking all commercial courses into account, at four-year intervals. Despite the introduction of the new course in 1926, males made up roughly 20 per cent of new commercial students in 1927 and 1931, as they had in 1923. It is only in 1935 that even a minor change in ratio is detectable.

Despite the apparent failure of the new course to alter significantly the gender ratio in the commercial department, it still may have helped with the symbolic status of the discipline, since the mere presence of this course on the books provided evidence for commercial studies' importance. In an attempt to raise the status of commercial classes generally, the staff at the Technical School pointed to gender differences in education, and in particular, to the presence of young men in segregated classes. By contrast, the school did not refer to other commercial courses as being 'for girls', indicating the low status of a female clientele, and leaving the impression that all commercial courses contained some males.

While the introduction of a specifically gender segregated course reveals an obvious attempt to manipulate student characteristics, the introduction of the special one-year course demands closer inspection. In fact, the special commercial course also sought to attract a new group of students – students with a different socio-economic background from those normally associated with the Technical School. The move of the commercial department to the Technical School (a result of the decrease in status associated with the gender characteristics of students) had started a further round of devaluation associated with the socio-economic background of pupils; gender and class patterns began to interact in a vicious downward spiral. In the 1920s and 1930s, new patterns of attendance brought about by legislative and economic changes tied technical schools more and more firmly to a working-class student body, perceived to have less academic ability.[62]

The composition of London Technical School's student body differed dramatically from that of the more academically oriented Collegiate. A comparison of the occupational status of student families at the Collegiate Institute and the Technical School shows this discrepancy. Table 2 reveals that two-thirds of the pupils in the Collegiate came from families headed by men or women employed in white collar positions, while only a fifth of Technical

Table 2 Parental occupations (percentages), London secondary schools, 1922

	Collegiate Institute	*Technical High School*
Non-manual	66.3	21.5
Manual skilled	30.1	58.2
Manual unskilled	3.6	20.3
n	880	423

Source: Ontario, Minister of Education, *Annual Report* (1922: 228–9 and 260–1)

School pupils came from this group. The figures for manual occupations are reversed.[63]

One established at the Technical School, commercial studies drew from its pool of students. Table 3 identifies student socio-economic status on the basis of the parental occupation listed on student record cards from the Technical School. This table reveals the similarity in the socio–economic status of students in the two general courses. The data show that a slight difference in class characteristics of female students taking the general technical and commercial courses existed in 1927, but vanished thereafter. For 1931 and 1935, the patterns of representation seem almost identical. Thus, at least in the 1930s, class had no bearing on patterns of enrolment in the two general courses, and commercial studies thus suffered the double disability of a student body under-valued both in gender and in class terms.

The special one-year course sought to remedy this problem. Because the course demanded at least two years' high school standing for admission, it

Table 3 Socio-economic characteristics of female students in selected courses (column percentages)

	General technical	*General commercial*	*Special commercial*
1927			
Non-manual	19	30	53
Skilled manual	40	36	28
Unskilled manual	40	33	19
n	67	129	58
1931			
Non-manual	25	24	39
Skilled manual	37	38	42
Unskilled manual	38	38	19
n	92	105	69
1935			
Non-manual	30	33	60
Skilled manual	33	35	30
Unskilled manual	37	32	10
n	81	135	83

Source: LTCHS student record cards

enrolled only students who transferred from another secondary school, which meant in practice usually one of the Collegiate Institutes, though a few came from private schools or rural continuation schools. Many of the students entering this course had already achieved junior or senior matriculation; in a few cases, young women even attended this course after graduating from university.[64] The special commercial course thus drew students not from the general pool of students entering the Technical School, but from a pool of those who had entered the Collegiate Institutes or other secondary institutions.

The presence of the new group of students changed the socio-economic composition of the commercial department. Table 3 shows how the socio-economic status of these students contrasted with that of the students in the two general courses discussed above. Where the non-manual segment of the general courses varied between a fifth and a third of all students, in a special commercial course it varied from two-fifths to three-fifths. At its minimum, it still exceeded the maximum for either of the other two courses.

These two new courses, then, emerged at the technical school to help raise teachers' professional status; while doing so, the courses also increased lines of segregation within the student population based on ascribed, involuntary characteristics. The creation of a course restricted to males added to the formal distinction between the genders in school society. The special one-year course produced similar, if less obvious, effects. While the new course did succeed in attracting a more highly valued clientele, in doing so it created a new division in the student body, which corresponded to a difference in socio-economic status.

While the class-based segregation imposed by the new course did not upset proponents of social efficiency, it did mark an unintended, if acceptable, outcome. Although Beal himself did attempt to minimize the social distance between the special commercial pupils and those from the general courses by organizing school-wide recreational activities,[65] these social events did nothing more than mask the systematic stratification being worked at the level of curriculum.

As is so often the case in historical research, the authors have to wonder whether their edifice of argument and evidence appears to others as little more than a house of cards. Direct evidence supports the following assertions. First, during the period 1900–20, commercial studies in London, Ontario, suffered from a trend of increasing marginalization in the Collegiate Institute, which culminated in a transfer to the Technical High School – an institution with a much less enviable reputation. Second, this marginalization occurred at the same time that the subject's student body underwent a process of feminization. Third, at the Technical School, the commercial studies student body quickly became identical, in social class terms, to the technical student body, and different from that of the Collegiate Institute. Fourth, during 1923 and 1924 the school underwent a series of attacks led by the conservative local newspaper and City Council members. Fifth, soon after these attacks ended, school officials decided to introduce two new courses which made little difference to existing students. Sixth, the first of the new courses aimed to attract CI students and resulted in a different class composition in the student body. Seventh, the other new course aimed at attracting males, thus directly seeking to change the student body profile.

This chapter has tried to tie these seven phenomena together in one particular and specific sense by arguing for the importance of the notion of subject status. Since subject status played a major role in determining professional career status and prospects, the personal interests of commercial teachers demanded attempts to elevate the discipline's status. One way to do so involved changing the characteristics of the student body, since at this time subject status rested to a degree on the perceived value of the students enrolled. In particular, student social characteristics of gender and class acted as crucial determinants in setting the status of a particular subject. The curriculum change of the mid-1920s sought to achieve this restructuring.

In the end, the struggle for professional status resulted in a major increase in stratification and segregation in the Technical School. While educators acknowledged the gender segregation, the more circumspect class segregation provided similarly potent mechanisms for structuring student experience in the school. The result was a distinction by class and gender in the credentials students received from their secondary schooling. The fact that these changes took place under provincial authority seems to indicate that London's situation was far from unique, and might have reflected a province-wide concern with the status of commercial studies. This suggests strongly that the 1920s witnessed increased socio-economic segregation in secondary school commercial courses throughout Ontario – a conclusion which matches recent interpretations of the so-called 'vocational era' in the history of education.[66]

7 'Nations at Risk' and 'National Curriculum': Ideology and Identity

While a good deal of our curriculum study should be conducted, as in the case of the London Technical and Commercial High School, at the school and local level, other historical work is required to examine wider initiatives of a national and even global scope. In this chapter I focus on the phenomenon emergent in a number of countries of 'national curriculum'. My primary evidence is of the emergence of the national curriculum in the United Kingdom.[1] I focus on the antecedents to the national curriculum and the arguments and groups through which it has been promoted; the structures, rhetorical, financial and political, which have been established to support it; and finally the content, form and pedagogical assumptions embedded within it.

As in other countries, the national curriculum debate in the UK has been precipitated by a widespread, and largely correct, perception that the nation is threatened by economic decline. Rhetorically then, the national curriculum is presented as a part of the project of economic regeneration. Behind this broad objective, however, two other projects can be discerned: first, the reconstitution of older class-based British 'traditional' subjects;[2] second, a reassertion of the ideology and control of the nation-state.

A good deal of recent historical work has furthered our understanding of the origins of state schooling and curriculum. The common feature uniting the wide range of initiatives by states to fund and manage mass schooling was, these scholars argue, the endeavour of constructing a national polity; the power of the nation-state, it was judged, would be unified through the participation of the state's subjects in national projects. Central in this socialization into national identity was the project of mass state schooling. The sequences followed by those states promoting this national project of mass schooling were strikingly similar. Initially there was the promulgation of a national interest in mass education. Legislation to make schooling compulsory for all followed. To organize the system of mass schools, state departments or ministries of education were formed. State authority was then exercised over all schools – both 'autonomous' schools already existing and newly proliferating schools specifically organized or opened by the state.

If the central project behind the initiation of state schooling and state-prescribed curriculum was nation-building, this may partly explain the response to certain moral panics which are currently evident. Above all is the new sense of panic over the 'nation at risk', the title chosen for the major US report on education in 1983. The perception of national crisis is common among Western nation-states. Often the matter is presented as essentially economic: certain nations (e.g. the USA) are falling behind certain other nations (e.g. Japan) in terms of economic prosperity. But behind this specific economic rationale lie a range of further more fundamental issues which render 'nations at risk' and develop general legitimation crises. The globalization of economic life, and more particularly of communications, information and technology, poses enormous challenges to the existing modes of control and operation of nation-states. In this sense the pursuance of new centralized national curriculum might be seen as the response of the more economically endangered species among nations. Britain provides an interesting case of this kind of response.

Behind the myths projected by the current UK government and echoed by some of the more sympathetic newspapers and media, the UK economy remains under-capitalized and in many instances hopelessly uncompetitive. So much for the economic basis of the 'nation at risk'. But perhaps even more significant are the tendencies towards globalization of economic and social life. In the UK case this is rendered particularly acute by the impending full-scale integration into the European Community. Symbolically the Channel Tunnel will connect UK life with that in Europe. The 'island nation' will quite literally be opened up to subterranean entry. The fear of the nation being at risk no doubt explains the hysteria behind so much of the Thatcher government's response to European integration.[3] Pervasive in this response is the sense of a loss of control, a loss of national destiny and identity. The school curriculum provides one arena for reasserting control and for re-establishing national identity.

The move towards a national curriculum in the UK can be traced back to the late 1970s. The key item in UK postwar educational history was Prime Minister James Callaghan's Ruskin College (Oxford) Speech in 1976, referred to in Chapter 1. Here economic decline and an accelerating sense of national demise (the UK had joined the European Community in 1973) where attached to the decline in educational standards which, it was argued, had been fostered in comprehensive schools by the use of more 'progressive' methods. Callaghan's speech called for a 'Great Debate' on the UK's educational policies. Following this initiative, in 1977 a Green Paper, *Education in Schools: a Consultative Document*, was issued. The arguments for a common 'core' or a 'protected' element emerged. The principal points of concern appear to be:

(i)   the curriculum has become overcrowded; the timetable is overloaded, and the essentials are at risk;

(ii) variations in the approach to the curriculum in different schools can penalize a child simply because he or she has moved from one area to another;

(iii) even if the child does not move, variations from school to school may give rise to inequality of opportunities;

(iv) the curriculum in many schools is not sufficiently matched to life in a modern industrial society.

The Report adds:

Not all these comments may be equally valid, but it is clear that the time has come to try to establish generally accepted principles for the composition of the secondary curriculum for all pupils. This does not presuppose uniform answers: schools, pupils, and their teachers are different, and the curriculum should be flexible enough to reflect these differences. But there is a need to investigate the part which might be played by a 'protected' or 'core' element of the curriculum common to all schools. There are various ways this may be defined. Properly worked out, it can offer reassurances to employers, parents, and the teachers themselves, as well as a very real equality of opportunity for pupils.[4]

The emerging 'consensus' that there should be a 'core' curriculum was further promoted in the period after the election of a Conservative government under Margaret Thatcher in 1979. The 1980 consultative paper, *A Framework for the School Curriculum*, argued that:

In the course of the public and professional debate about the school curriculum a good deal of support has been found for the idea of identifying a 'core' or essential part of the curriculum which should be followed by all pupils according to their ability. Such a core, it is hoped, would ensure that all pupils, whatever else they do, at least get a sufficient grounding in the knowledge and skills which by common consent should form part of the equipment of the educated adult.

Thus expressed, the idea may appear disarmingly simple; but as soon as it is critically examined a number of supplementary questions arise. For example, should the core be defined as narrowly as possible, or should it, for the period of compulsory schooling at least, cover a large part of the individual's curriculum? Should it be expressed in terms of the traditional school subjects, or in terms of educational objectives which may be attained through the medium of various subjects, appropriately taught? The difficulties and uncertainties attached to the application of the core concept do not mean, however, that it may not be a useful one in carrying forward the public debate about the curriculum to the point at which its results can be of practical benefit to the schools.[5]

These difficulties notwithstanding, from this point on there was a fairly consistent drive to establish a core curriculum. Following the Conservative Party's third election success in 1987, this curriculum was established as a new 'national curriculum', comprising the 'core subjects' of mathematics, English and science, and the 'foundation subjects' of history, geography, technology, music, art and physical education.

Alongside this specification of subject titles was a panoply of major new central powers over the school curriculum. The Secretary of State for Education and Science now has responsibility for specifying attainment targets, programmes of study and assessment procedures for each specified subject area. It should be noted that these are powers for very detailed prescription indeed, they are not the powers of merely a general overview. Written into the Parliamentary legislation is the obligation to assess pupils on the curriculum studied at ages 7, 11, 14 and 16. In addition, a National Curriculum Council and a School Examinations and Assessment Council[6] have been set up to advise on the research, development and monitoring procedures required.

The styling of the new curriculum specifications as 'national', the composition of subjects included and the wide-ranging new power for governmental agencies suggest three levels of enquiry in coming to understand this new initiative. First there is the need for further enquiry of the theme with which we began: the relationship of these curriculum initiatives to national economic regeneration and national identity. Second, the focus on a small number of traditional subjects raises the question of the social antecedents of this choice: we need to analyse the social and cultural, as well as political, choices that underpin the new national curriculum. Third, the initiative needs to be scrutinized in terms of the changing modalities of government control, which are so clearly pronounced.

The national curriculum and national identity

The national curriculum has been initiated with pronouncements casting national regeneration in terms of links to the economy, industry and commerce, in particular the so-called 'wealth creating' sector. Yet in practice the balance of subjects in the national curriculum suggests that questions of national identity and control have been pre-eminent, rather than industrial or commercial requirements. For example, information technology (as distinct from versions of design and technology) has been largely omitted, while history has been embraced as a 'foundation subject', even though it is quite clearly a subject in decline within the schools.

The reasons for favouring history while omitting more commercially 'relevant' subjects are intriguing. On the face of it, this pattern of prioritizing might seem encouraging: sponsoring liberal education and humanist study over more narrow utilitarian concerns, favouring education over training. Regrettably this does not seem to be the case. History has, I believe, been chosen to revive and refocus national identity and ideology.

The recent National Curriculum History Group Interim Report provides information on the new curriculum proposals for school history. First, the report confirms that before the revival initiated by the incorporation in the national curriculum, history was a subject in decline: 'It now has a tenuous place in the primary curriculum and it is under threat in a growing number of secondary schools, both in terms of the number of pupils taking it, and as a coherent, rigorous and free-standing course of study.'[7] One of the reasons for the progressive decline of history has been the growth of social studies and sociology. The latter subject is a very popular examination subject, but has been omitted in the national curriculum in favour of reviving history. The questions remain as to why history has been so favoured.

The Interim Report provides some evidence on this issue, for the national curriculum in history will have some distinctive features. At the core will be UK history, which overall will take up 40 per cent of the timetable. 'This figure, however, is slightly misleading because children at key stage one infant level will study UK history almost exclusively, while pupils in the early years of the secondary school will study it as a core subject for just one-third of the time earmarked for history.'[8] The focus of the national curriculum on British history in the formative early years of schooling indicates a wish to inculcate at an early stage a sense of national identity. This desire for a major and increased UK dimension in history has plainly come from within the government. We are told, for instance, that:

> The issue which has hitherto aroused the most controversy is the Minister's insistence that the group should increase the proportion of British history for secondary pupils. At the moment, the group is planning to devote only one-third of the syllabus to British history as a compulsory subject for 11- to 14-year-olds. This figure rises slightly to two-fifths for 14- to 16-year-olds. Mr. MacGregor wants British history to be taught for at least 50% of the time devoted to history in secondary schools.[9]

John MacGregor, appointed by Prime Minister Thatcher as the Secretary of State for Education and Science, was clear where the government's priorities lay. Certainly the revival of UK history seems unrelated to any strong desires among history teachers themselves, where many disagreements have been voiced. These disagreements have even been voiced inside the select curriculum working group: 'At the heart of these disagreements on historical knowledge, British history and chronology, is the lingering fear among some numbers of the group particularly those who are teachers or educationists that the history curriculum will be dominated by rigid external testing and rote learning of famous dates in British history.'[10]

National curriculum and social prioritizing

The styling of the curriculum as 'national' begs a number of questions about which nation is being referred to, for the UK is a nation sharply divided by social class, by race, by gender, by region and by country. One of the shorthands for Conservative criticism of what a French Prime Minister has called the UK government's 'social cruelty' has been a reference to the danger of creating 'two nations'. This refers to the UK phenomenon of there being two recognizably different constituencies or nations inside the UK's borders: one nation which is richer and more secure and often resides in the so-called 'Home Counties' of south-eastern England, and the other nation which is less well-endowed, primarily working class and lives in that 'other country' beyond south-eastern England. In truth, of course, the UK comprises a range of communities, segmented by class, race, gender, region and country; there are in fact far more than two nations.

Hence, in examining the national curriculum as a social construction, it is important to establish whether the different groups that comprise 'the nation' are being treated equally, or whether processes of social prioritizing can be discerned. In this section, by way of exemplification, I focus mainly on the issue of social class, but work urgently needs to be undertaken around issues of race, gender, region and country. In each of these cases the construction of particular priorities and the simultaneous silencing of multiple other claims needs to be painstakingly examined.

The pattern of secondary schooling has a long history but a crucial watershed was the 1902 Education Act and the subsequent issue of the Secondary Regulations in 1904. At the turn of the century a number of alternative versions of secondary schooling were vying with each other. The well-established public schools and grammar schools carried the highest status and catered for the more elite social groups through a traditional classical curriculum, but increasingly the school boards administering local schools were providing education for secondary age pupils. In these schools a more vocational curriculum, covering commercial, technical and scientific subjects, was provided for a predominantly working class clientele (as we have seen in Chapters 6 and 7, a pattern somewhat echoed in Ontario at the same time).

The 1902 Education Act and the Secondary Regulations therefore arbitrated between these two traditions. Ryder and Silver have judged that the 1902 Act ensured that 'whatever developments in secondary education might occur, it should be within a single system in which the dominant values should resemble those of the traditional grammar school and its curriculum'.[11] Likewise, Eaglesham judged that:

> These regulations were the work of a number of officials and inspectors of the Board. It may be argued that they gave a balanced curriculum. They certainly effectively checked any tendencies to technical or vocational bias in the secondary schools. They made them schools fit only for a selected few. Moreover they proclaimed for all to see the Board's interest in the literary and classical sides of secondary education. For the future the pattern of English culture must come not from Leeds and West Ham but from Eton and Winchester.[12]

While these two quotes present grammar and public curricula in too monolithic a manner the general point can be summarized in this way: 'Secondary education was in 1904 given so academic a curriculum that it suited only a few.'[13] In this manner the settlement of 1902–4 chose the historical legacy and curriculum aimed at certain groups over that aimed at other groups and legislated that this model should constitute the secondary school curriculum. The

1904 Secondary Regulations outline clear guidelines (for details see Chapter 1); we then see curriculum as social prioritizing.

The division of post-primary schooling between public schools, grammar schools and other schools pre-eminently for the working class, the elementary schools and subsequently secondary modern schools, survived into the period following the Second World War. Opposition to the selective examination for deciding who went to grammar school, the so-called eleven-plus, grew and some experiments in comprehensive or multilateral schooling began in the 1940s. In 1964 a Labour government was returned, and began dismantling the existing divisive system and introducing comprehensive schools.

The implications of this change for the curriculum were substantial, and a range of curriculum reform projects were initiated through the Schools Council for Curriculum and Examinations, founded in 1964. While the comprehensive schools initially derived their main curriculum areas from the grammar schools, these reform projects sought to apply seriously the logic of comprehensive school reform to curriculum reform. Plainly, without curriculum reform organizational reform was of severely limited significance.

Rubinstein and Simon summarize the climate of educational reform in 1972 following the raising of the school-leaving age to sixteen, and the rapid growth of the comprehensive system:

> The content of the curriculum is now under much discussion, and comprehensive schools are participating actively in the many curriculum reform schemes launched by the Schools Council and Nuffield. The tendency is towards the development of the interdisciplinary curricula, together with the use of the resources approach to learning, involving the substitution of much group and individual work for the more traditional forms of class teaching. For these new forms of organising and stimulating learning mixed ability grouping often provides the most appropriate method; and partly for this reason the tendency is towards the reduction of streaming and class teaching. This movement in itself promotes new relations between teachers and pupils, particularly insofar as the teacher's role is changing from that of ultimate authority to that of motivating, facilitating and structuring the pupils' own discovery and search for knowledge.[14]

The belief that rapid curriculum reform, with a range of associated political and pedagogical implications, was well under way was commonly held at this time. Kerr asserted in 1968 that 'at the practical and organisational levels, the new curricula promise to revolutionise English education'.[15]

At precisely the time Kerr was talking, new forces were seeking to defend, and if possible reinvigorate, the old grammar school subjects. These were presented as the 'traditional' subjects. We have discussed in Chapter 1 how this campaign culminated in the national curriculum but it is important to grasp that this reassertion of a subject-based curriculum is part of a broader strategy of reconstitution. Moreover, the re-establishment of traditional subjects is taking place at the expense of many of those new subject areas devised specifically to sponsor and promote learning across the full range of the comprehensive school: social studies, environmental studies, general science, urban studies, community studies and so on. These subjects had sought to develop new forms of connectedness to the interests and experiences of the pupils of the comprehensive school. The national curriculum pronounces that the approach can now only take place at the margins and that the core curriculum will once again be those subjects 'traditionally' taught since their 'establishment' in 1904.

A comparison with the Secondary Regulations in 1904 shows the extent to which a patterning of schooling has been reconstituted in this new political settlement called the national curriculum:

1904	1988
English	English
Maths	Maths
Science	Science
History	History
Geography	Geography
Physical exercise	Physical education
Drawing	Art
Foreign language	Modern foreign language
Manual work ⎫ Domestic subjects ⎭	Technology
(Music added soon afterwards)	Music

The similarity between 1904 and 1988 questions the rhetoric of 'a major new initiative' employed by the government, and points to some historical continuities in social and political purpose and priorities. The 1904 Regulations embodied that curriculum historically offered to the grammar school clientele as opposed to the curriculum being developed in the Board Schools and aimed primarily at the working classes: one segment or vision of the nation was being favoured at the expense of another. In the intervening period more egalitarian impulses brought about the creation of comprehensive schools, where children of all classes came together under one roof. This in turn led to a range of curriculum reforms that sought to redefine and challenge the hegemony of the grammar school curriculum.

Seeking in turn to challenge and redirect these reforms and intentions, the political right has argued for the rehabilitation of the 'traditional' (i.e. grammar school) subjects. The national curriculum can be seen as a political statement of the victory of the forces and intentions representing these political groups. A particular vision and a preferred segment of the nation has therefore been reinstated and prioritized, and legislated as 'national'.

The historical continuities evident in the national curriculum have been commented on in a number of places. For instance, *The Times Educational Supplement* stated that 'the first thing to say about this whole exercise is that it unwinds 80 years of English (and Welsh) educational history. It is a case of go back to Go.'[16] In writing of the National Curriculum Project, Moon and Mortimore commented:

> The legislation, and the much-criticized consultative document that preceded it, present the curriculum in needlessly rather restricted terms. Thus the primary curriculum was put forward as if it were no more than a presecondary preparation (like the worst sort of 'prep school'). All the positive aspects of British primary schooling so valued by HMI and the Select Committee of the House of Commons and so praised by many foreign commentators were ignored.
>
> The secondary curriculum, in turn, appears to be based on the curriculum of a typical 1960s grammar school. We would not take issue with the subjects included, but we believe that such a curriculum misses out a great deal. Information technology, electronics, statistics, personal, social and careers education have all been omitted. Yet, surely, these are just the areas that are likely to be of importance for the future lives of many pupils?[17]

The national curriculum, then, can be seen as a response to a 'nation at risk' at two levels. First, there is the general sense of the nation-state being in economic decline and subject to globalization and to amalgamation in the wider European Community. There the response is paradoxical. Nation-building curricula are often favoured over commercially 'relevant' curricula. The solution may therefore exacerbate the problem. Further economic 'decline' may follow, leading to even more desperate attempts to reassert national identity. Second, given that the UK is clearly a divided nation, investigation of the national curriculum allows insights into precisely *which* nation is at risk. It would seem it is the elite and middle class groups that were perceived as 'at risk'. For it is these groups that have the greatest historical connections to the 'traditional subjects': these subjects have been revived and reinstated in the national curriculum.

The perception of nations at risk and social groups at risk has provided one further source of support for developing the powers of central state over the school curriculum. This is the third level at which the national curriculum is significant. In the central project of rebuilding the nation-state, the issue of re-establishing national identity and ideology has been dealt with, but there remains the issue of rebuilding the power of the nation-state itself.

National curriculum and national power

In postwar Britain the national state's powers over education were increasingly devolved to local education authorities (LEAs). This made the schools more responsive to the local 'communities' than to 'the nation'. In addition the teachers' unions were able to assert a growing influence over issues of curriculum and assessment reform. As we have noted, this led some comprehensive schools to develop more comprehensive curricula, which moved beyond the

1904-style academic curriculum 'suited to only a few'. The national state's loss of control, specifically loss of control over curriculum, therefore led to patterns of prioritizing which went a long way from the political settlement enshrined in the 1904 Regulations: the so-called traditional subjects. This loss of control therefore threatened those groups who had benefited from this political settlement. The social prioritization so well-established in the early twentieth century was plainly under attack. In short, the 'nation' as represented in these privileged groups was 'at risk'.

Of course, reasserting the primacy of curriculum as a vehicle for the education of the elite and custodial classes entirely fits a version of nation-building. These leadership and professional groups are precisely those who will rule and administer the nation – it is consistent to remake the curriculum in their image and reconstruct schools as mechanisms for the selection of this national meritocracy. But the form of this national reconstruction at the level of curriculum, of course, reflects the existing perception and situation of the 'nation'. Plainly, at this point in its history the UK nation-state reflects the postwar period of precipitous decline. Since 1945 the large aspirations of the nation-state as a major imperial power, a major player on the world stage, have had to be severely redefined. A particularly problematic aspect of this imperial angst had been how to deal with the plurality of other cultures. This concern is often wished off into the field of 'multicultural studies' but is integral to notions of identity and democracy in general. Alongside ideological decline has been a savage experience of economic decline. In both these aspects of decline the British establishment, the elite and the professions, has been implicated. As a result, any campaign to reconstruct and revive the nation would have to respond to this experience of precipitous decline. The particular version of nation-building through curriculum is therefore likely to reflect this perception.

The definition of a central curriculum could in fact take a number of forms, but there are two major directions. One version would specify a common set of goals and objectives and a certain amount of common content. In this version the teachers and students are allowed some flexibility, and a degree of accommodation with local conditions and concerns is both expected and encouraged. This version of central curriculum would have resonated well with the experience of the UK educational system in the twentieth century. A second version of central curriculum would prescribe in detail what is to be taught, learned and tested. There would be little allowance for choice on the part of teachers and students. One caricature of this version would be the mythical French Minister of Education, who could look at his watch and say what every child in France was studying at any given time. This version of common curricula would go against the grain of twentieth-century UK experience.

That the 1988 UK national curriculum in fact represents the second model of central curriculum says a good deal. It reflects the response of a political establishment that has experienced more than four decades of precipitous and accelerating political and economic decline. In such circumstances the replay of paranoid fears within the domain of the school curriculum seems an understandable, if indirect, response.

The unprecedented expansion of powers over the school curriculum has not gone unnoticed or unchallenged. The Cabinet's intention in the report on history has led the Historical Association, an august and conservative body representing history teachers, to question whether the government has any 'constitutional right' for such detailed intervention.

The major expansion of state power over the curriculum and over assessment leads to a parallel diminution in the teachers' power and therefore has associated implications for pedagogy. At one level the new power over curriculum and the battery of tests represent a substantial push to make the details of teachers' work accountable to the state. The structure of the 1960s, where teachers were judged to have superior expertise in assessing the educational needs of their pupils, has been rapidly dismantled.

Much of the commentary on the new national curriculum has been sympathetic and optimistic about the results of the expansion of state power. For instance, *The Times* carried an editorial on the passing of the 'True Education Bill', which argued that 'most important, a national curriculum, accompanied by attainment targets and tests at key ages, will ensure that a large proportion of young people leave school literate, numerate, and more broadly educated than they are now. In short, standards will rise. That is because teachers will have a clearer idea of what is expected of them.'[18] In short, greater accountability (and less power over definition) leads to clearer objectives and better work habits. This is a crude simplification employing an almost Taylorist optimism about a strategy for tackling a most complex enterprise.

Lessons from previous historical episodes must be treated with considerable caution, for we are not comparing like with like. Yet so clear have been the experiences of teachers and taught in the face of nineteenth-century government interventions in matters of curriculum and assessment that the pious simplifications behind *The Times*'s viewpoint should be severely scrutinized. For it may not be the case that standards will rise; rather morale will fall. (Indeed, by 1993 this is exactly what *The Times* was reporting and asserting – four years would seem a very short learning curve.)

A major experiment in state control of school curricula was conducted in the years 1862 to 1895. The teachers were made subject to a system of 'payment by results': teachers' pay was linked to pupils' results in school examinations. E. G. A. Holmes, a school inspector at the time, has left a detailed commentary on the results of this experiment. He notes that from 1862 to 1895 'a considerable part of the Grant received by each school was paid on the results of a yearly examination held by HM [Her Majesty's] Inspector on an elaborate syllabus, formulated by the Department and binding on all schools alike.' The results of this mechanism were clear. 'On the official report which followed this examination depended the reputation and financial prosperity of the school, and the reputation and financial prosperity of the teacher.'[19] The government had therefore established deliberate and detailed control over curriculum and assessment and thereby over the teacher and student. Power was thus established, but what of the 'side-effects' on education? On this Holmes was adamant:

The consequent pressure on the teacher to exert himself was well-nigh irresistible; and he had no choice but to transmit that pressure to his subordinates and his pupils. The result was that in those days the average school was a hive of industry.

But it was also a hive of misdirected energy. The State, in prescribing a syllabus which was to be followed, in all the subjects of instruction, by all the schools in the country, without regard to local or personal consider-ations, was guilty of one capital offence. It did all his thinking for the teacher. It told him in precise detail what he was to do each year in each 'Standard', how he was to handle each subject, and how far he was to go in it; what width of ground he was to cover; what amount of knowledge, what degree of accuracy was required for a 'pass'. In other words, it provided him with his ideals, his general conceptions, his more immedi-ate aims, his schemes of work; and if it did not control his methods in all their details, it gave him (by implication) hints and suggestions with regard to these on which he was not slow to act; for it told him that the work done in each class and each subject would be tested at the end of each year by a careful examination of each individual child; and it was inevitable that in his endeavour to adapt his teaching to the type of question which his experience of the yearly examination led him to expect, he should gradually deliver himself, mind and soul, into the hands of the officials of the Department, the officials at Whitehall who framed the yearly syllabus, and the officials in the various districts who examined on it.

What the Department did to the teacher, it compelled him to do to the child. The teacher who is the slave of another's will cannot carry out his instructions except by making his pupils the slaves of his own will. The teacher who has been deprived by his superiors of freedom, initiative, and responsibility, cannot carry out his instructions except by depriving his pupils of the same vital qualities. The teacher who, in response to the deadly pressure of a cast-iron system, has become a creature of habit and routine, cannot carry out his instructions except by making his pupils as helpless and as puppet-like as himself.

But it is not only because mechanical obedience is fatal, in the long run, to mental and spiritual growth, that the regulation of elementary or any other grade of education by a uniform syllabus is to be deprecated. It is also because a uniform syllabus is, in the nature of things, a bad syllabus, and because the degree of its badness varies directly with the arc of the sphere of educational activity that comes under its control.[20]

Holmes provided more details of the working of a system of state prescription of syllabus and control of examinations:

It was preordained, then, that the syllabuses which the Department iss-ued, year by year, in the days of payment by results should have few merits and many defects. Yet even if, by an unimaginable miracle, they had all been educationally sound, the mere fact that all the teachers in

England had to work by them would have made them potent agencies for evil. To be in bondage to a syllabus is a misfortune for a teacher, and a misfortune for the school that he teaches. To be in bondage to a syllabus which is binding on all schools alike is of all misfortunes the gravest. Or if there is a graver, it is the fate that befell the teachers of England under the old regime – the fate of being in bondage to a syllabus which was bad both because it had to come down to the level of the least fortunate school and the least capable teacher, and also because it was the outcome of ignorance, inexperience, and bureaucratic self-satisfaction.

Of the evils that are inherent in the examination system as such of its tendency to arrest growth, to deaden life, to paralyse the higher faculties, to externalize what is inward, to materialize what is spiritual, to involve education in an atmosphere of unreality and self-deception I have already spoken at some length. In the days of payment by results various circumstances conspired to raise those evil tendencies to the highest imaginable 'power'. When inspectors ceased to examine (in the stricter sense of the word), they realised what infinite mischief the yearly examination had done. The children, the majority of whom were examined in reading and dictation out of their own reading-books (two or three in number, as the case might be), were drilled in the contents of those books until they knew them almost by heart. In arithmetic they worked abstract sums, in obedience to formal rules, day after day, and month after month; and they were put up to various tricks and dodges which would, it was hoped, enable them to know by what precise rules the various questions on the arithmetic cards were to be answered. They learned a few lines of poetry by heart and committed all the 'meanings and allusions' to memory, with the probable result – so sickening must the process have been – that they hated poetry for the rest of their lives. In geography, history, and grammar they were the victims of unintelligent oral cram, which they were compelled, under pains and penalties, to take in and retain till the examination day was over, their ability to disgorge it on occasion being periodically tested by the teacher. And so with the other subjects. Not a thought was given, except in a small minority of the schools, to the real training of the child, to the fostering of his mental (and other) growth. To get him through the yearly examination by hook or by crook was the one concern of the teacher. As profound distrust of the teacher was the basis of the policy of the Department, so profound distrust of the child was the basis of the policy of the teacher. To leave the child to find out anything for himself, to work out anything for himself, to think out anything for himself, would have been regarded as a proof of incapacity, not to say insanity, on the part of the teacher, and would have led to results which, from the 'percentage' point of view, would probably have been disastrous.[21]

In fact the experience of this episode of state intervention had long-lasting effects. In 1944, when the government was drawing up the influential Education Act of that year, James Chuter Ede, parliamentary secretary to the Minister, said in a speech to the House:

> there is not one curriculum for every child, but every child must be a separate problem for the teacher. The teacher is the servant of the State, and I hope that no one will say that the State should lay down the curriculum of the schools. Some of us were brought up under the old payment-by-results system, and were the time earlier, I could amuse the House with descriptions that some of my Hon. friends know would be no caricature of the way in which State control of the curriculum prevented the development of a wise and sound system of education.[22]

Holmes and Chuter Ede then warn us of some of the dangers that attended a 'national curriculum and assessment' strategy. But the implications for teachers and particularly pupils are of profound concern. The development of attitudes of 'mechanical obedience' strike at the very heart of the 'democratic' system of governance. This matter assumes great importance at a time when there is widespread comment in the UK about the absence of constitutional rights and the consequent possibility of substantial erosion of 'traditional' rights by more authoritarian government, whether of the right (as at the moment) or of the left. The link between the national curriculum and mechanical obedience therefore highlights a major problem with regard to the education of pupils with the capacity to be functioning citizens in a democracy. I find the following statement about 'the erosion of British liberty' particularly chilling in this light: 'Britons have been schooled to think of themselves as subjects, not citizens; as people with freedoms granted by government, not with rights guaranteed against government interference.'[23] The traditional school subject based national curriculum plays a key role in constructing the particular subjectivities of subjects in this sense.[24]

Seen in this light the political project underpinning the national curriculum assumes a further dimension, for the hidden curriculum of the national curriculum is a reassertion of the power of the state in nation-building. This project is diametrically opposed to the alternative project of educating pupils, from a plurality of cultures, for active citizenship in a democracy. The history of mass mechanical obedience as a bedrock for nation-building is well known, but it leads not to democracy but to totalitarianism.

Conclusion

The introduction of the national curriculum in the UK has been linked to the problems of national economic decline and a belief that curriculum coordination will aid a project of national economic regeneration. Behind the rhetorical priority given to economic revival, two other agendas have been discerned.

The first is the reconstitution of a traditional subjects-based curriculum. These traditional subjects evoke a past 'golden age' when schooling was selective and people 'knew their station'. A number of empirical studies have pointed up the links between traditional subjects and social class.[25] The obsessive presentism of many of the current government initiatives has successfully obscured this deeply embedded connectedness, which is of course relevant to the present and future of the UK as a class society.

In the development of this commentary for a global audience, it is important to note the distinctiveness and strength of UK class politics. For instance, in the USA at the moment a debate is underway about defining a national curriculum comprising traditional subjects. However, the intention, at least one important intention, is to provide rigorous academic subject-based courses of study covering curriculum content and form which will appeal to *all* children. Hence, the pattern of state and class-formation in the USA means that a national curriculum initiative will have sharply different resonances from those in a somewhat obsolescent class-based society like the UK. (This is not, of course, to say that an initiative in the USA will not have powerful implications for matters of class, race and gender.) Moreover, the patterns of civic culture, citizenship education and constitutional rights are sharply different in the UK and the USA, so that once again a national curriculum will be likely to affect the two societies differently.

The second agenda in the UK is one of establishing new modalities of control over schooling on behalf of the nation-state. These new modalities will allow detailed control to be exercised over the school curriculum, in terms of content, form and assessment. In the UK this would seem a late and somewhat desperate attempt at nation-building, in terms of both nation-state governance and the partial propagation through curriculum of national ideologies, selective memories and images. It would seem possible that declining nations in their post-imperial phase have nowhere to go but to retreat into the bunker of the school curriculum. In this case, in particular, there may well be some lessons for the USA.

8 Studying Curriculum: Social Constructionist Perspectives[1]

As has been noted and illustrated throughout this book, one of the perennial problems of studying curriculum is that it is a multifaceted concept, constructed, negotiated and renegotiated at a variety of levels and in a variety of arenas. This elusiveness has no doubt contributed to the rise of theoretical and overarching perspectives and discourses in educational study, particularly the organizational and psychological, as well as more technical or scientific perspectives and discourses. These approaches have been criticized recurrently because they do violence to the practical essentials of curriculum as conceived of and realized. Hence, we need to move firmly and sharply away from these decontextualized modes of analysis: away from technical, rational or scientific management models; away from unproblematic belief in the 'objectives game'. To develop a more complex sense of the enterprise means that we must embrace fully a scholarly focus on *curriculum as social construction*, first at the level of prescription itself, but also at the levels of process, practice and discourse.

Curriculum as prescription

The primacy of the ideology of curriculum as prescription (CAP) can be evidenced in even a cursory glimpse at the curriculum literature. This view of curriculum develops from a belief that we can dispassionately define the main ingredients of the course of study and then proceed to teach the various segments and sequences in systematic turn. Despite the obvious simplicity, not to say crudity, of this view, the 'objectives game' is still, if not the only game in town, certainly the main game. There may be many reasons for this continuing predominance, but explanatory potential is not, I think, one of the factors.

Curriculum as prescription supports important mystiques about state schooling and society. Most notably, CAP supports the mystique that expertise and control reside within central governments, educational bureaucracies or university communities. As we saw in Chapter 7, when national groups and governments feel threatened this mystique becomes an important bulwark against an impending sense of disorder, disarray and decline. Providing nobody exposes this mystique, the two worlds of 'prescriptive rhetoric' and 'schooling as practice' can coexist. Both sides benefit from such peaceful coexistence. The agencies of CAP are seen to be 'in control' and the schools are seen to be 'delivering' (and can carve out a good degree of autonomy if they accept the rules). Curriculum prescriptions thereby set certain parameters – although transgression and occasional transcendence are permissible as long as the rhetoric of prescription and management is not challenged.

Of course there are costs of complicity in accepting the myth of prescription: above all these involve, in various ways, acceptance of established modes of power relations. Perhaps most importantly the people intimately connected with the day-to-day social construction of curriculum and schooling – teachers – are thereby effectively disenfranchised in the 'discourse of schooling'. To continue to exist, teachers' day-to-day power must remain unspoken and unrecorded. This is one price of complicity: day-to-day power and autonomy for schools and for teachers are dependent on continuing to accept the fundamental lie.

With regard to curriculum studies the costs of complicity are ultimately catastrophic, for the historic compromise we have described has led to the displacement of the mainstream of a whole field of study. It has led to the directing of scholarship into fields which service the mystique of central and/or bureaucratic control. The indicator of this complicity is the thoroughgoing historical amnesia of the curriculum field (see Chapter 1), to which, it is argued, social constructionist study, among other initiatives, will provide both an antidote and a challenge. At one level the denial of history, of social constructionist perspectives, is the denial of agency, especially teacher and pupil agency.

Towards a social constructionist programme of study

CAP and major reactions to CAP share one characteristic, namely a concern to develop models of 'idealized practice' (see Chapter 2).[2] Both models are concerned with what *ought* to be happening in schools, 'our commitment to what should be'. As Westbury argues, this can lead to 'meliorism'. It is thus important to restate the problems of CAP: not only that the focus is solely on prescription but that the kind of focus is decontextualized. We need an understanding of how curriculum prescriptions are in fact socially constructed for use in schools: studies of the actual development of courses of study, of national curriculum plans, of subject syllabuses and so on. Thus the problem, as we restate it, is not the *fact* of the focus on prescription, but the *singular* nature of that focus and the *kind* of focus thereby involved. What we require is a combined approach: a focus on the construction of prescriptive curricula and policy coupled with an analysis of the negotiations and realization of that prescribed curriculum, focusing on the essentially dialectical relationship of the two.

We want, in short, the story of action within a theory of context – to move a step back towards the centre following the moves of Schwab and some curriculum reformers to embrace the 'practical' terrain. Their reaction, I have argued, was too extreme a reaction, albeit understandable at the time. Since prescription continues (and, given the current centralist thrust in, for example, the UK, will strengthen) we need to understand social construction of curricula at the levels of prescription *and* process *and* practice *and* discourse. What is required is indeed to understand the practical but to locate this understanding within a further exploration of the contextual parameters of practice.

Social constructionist perspectives seek a reintegrated focus for studies of curriculum by moving away from a singular focus, whether on idealized practice or actual practice, towards the development of data on social construction at both preactive and interactive levels. At this point in time the most significant lacuna for such a reconceptualized programme of study is historical study of the social construction of school curricula. We know very little about how the subjects and themes prescribed in schools originate, how they are promoted and redefined, and how they metamorphose. We do know, however, that *preactive* construction of the school curriculum takes place at a number of levels: the prescriptions and dictates issued by central states and provincial and local bureaucracies; the prescriptions at the level of individual institutions; the mediated prescriptions at subject department level; finally, and importantly, the prescriptions and preparations of curriculum by individual classroom teachers. The preactive level of curriculum construction is then a major chain of agenda-setting for schooling and calls out for detailed study.

Work on the history and sociology of the social construction of school curricula is therefore a vital prerequisite for reconceptualized curriculum study. Fortunately, a good deal of work has been undertaken in the past decade which is coming to fruition. The series 'Studies in Curriculum History' now comprises a range of volumes that provide a wide range of different studies of the social construction of school curricula. But importantly, other work, especially in North America, extends this initiative and develops our understanding of the contestation that has surrounded the development of prescriptive curricula.

Studying the social construction of the curriculum

The task now being undertaken by scholars in a wide range of settings is to revive and reconstitute the role of historical and sociological methods in the study of curriculum and to rearticulate a mode of study for carrying further our understanding of the social construction of the school curriculum and of school subjects.

In *School Subjects and Curriculum Change*, first published in 1983, I looked at the history of three subjects: geography, biology and environmental studies.[3] Each of the subjects followed a similar evolutionary profile and this initial work allowed a series of hypotheses to be developed about the way that status and resources, the structuration of school subjects, push school subject knowledge in particular directions: towards the embrace of what I call the 'academic tradition'. Following this work a new series, 'Studies in Curriculum History', was launched. In the first volume, *Social Histories of the Secondary Curriculum*,[4] work is collected together on a wide range of subjects: classics (Stray), English (Ball), science (Waring, who had written an earlier germinal study on Nuffield science), domestic subjects (Purvis), religious education (Bell), social studies (Franklin and Whitty) and modern languages (Radford). These studies reflect a growing interest in the history of curriculum and, besides elucidating the symbolic drift of school knowledge towards the academic tradition, raise central questions about past and current explanations of school subjects whether they be sociological or philosophical. Other work in the series 'Studies in Curriculum History' has looked in detail at particular subjects. In 1985, McCulloch, Layton and Jenkins produced *Technological Revolution?*[5] This book examines the politics of school science and technology curriculum in England and Wales since the Second World War and was followed by Gary McCulloch's study, *The Secondary Technical School*.[6] Associated work by Brian Woolnough[7] has looked at the history of physics teaching in schools in the period 1960–85. Another area of emerging work is the history of school mathematics: Cooper's book *Renegotiating Secondary School Mathematics*[8] looks at the fate of a number of traditions within mathematics and articulates a model for the redefinition of school subject knowledge; Bob Moon's book *The 'New Maths' Curriculum Controversy*[9] meanwhile looks at the relationship between maths in England and the USA and has some very interesting work on the dissemination of textbooks.

Emerging work in the USA has also begun to focus on the evolution of the school curriculum studies in historical manner. H. M. Kliebard's seminal *The Struggle for the American Curriculum 1893–1958*[10] discerns a number of the dominant traditions within the school curriculum. The book also comes to the intriguing conclusion that by the end of the period covered the traditional school subject remained 'an impregnable fortress'. But Kliebard's work does not take us into the detail of school life. In this respect Barry Franklin's book, *Building the American Community*,[11] provides us with some valuable insights in a case study of Minneapolis. Here we seen the vital negotiation from curriculum ideas, the terrain of Kliebard's work, towards implementation as school practice. In addition, a collection of papers put together by Tom Popkewitz[12] looks at the historical aspects of a range of subjects: early education (Bloch), art (Freedman), reading and writing (Monagha and Saul), biology (Rosenthal and Bybee), mathematics (Stanic), social studies (Lybarger), special education (Franklin and Sleeter), socialist curriculum (Teitelbaum) and a study of Ruggs textbooks (Kliebard and Wegner).

In Canada, curriculum history has been launched as a field, most notably by George Tomkins' pioneering work *A Common Countenance*.[13] This book studies the patterns of curriculum stability and change in a range of school subjects over the past two centuries throughout Canada. The book has stimulated a wide range of important new work of curriculum history; for instance, Rowell and Gaskell's[14] very generative study of the history of school physics. The

Rowell and Gaskell piece provides one important case study in the book *International Perspectives in Curriculum History*,[15] which seeks to bring together some of the more important work emerging in different countries on curriculum history. Besides some of the work already noted by Stanic, Moon, Franklin, McCulloch, Bell and Gaskell, there are important articles on Victorian school science by Hodson, on science education by Louis Smith, on English in the Norwegian common school by Gundem, and on the development of senior school geography in West Australia by Marsh.

Other work has begun to go beyond traditional school subjects to look at broader topics. For example, Peter Cunningham's book looks at curriculum change in the primary school in Britain since 1945.[16] P. W. Musgrave's book, *Whose Knowledge?*,[17] is a case study of the Victoria University Examinations Board from 1964 to 1979. Here historical work begins to elucidate the change from curriculum content to examinable content, which is such an important part of understanding the way that status and resources are apportioned within the school.

Recent work has begun to explore gender patterns in curriculum history. Jane Bernard Powers's excellent study *The Girl Question in Education*[18] is a pioneering work in this regard. Likewise, work is beginning on the modernist construction of curriculum as a world movement. The work of John Meyer and colleagues, *School Knowledge for the Masses*,[19] provides a path-breaking study of national primary curricula categories in the twentieth century throughout the world.

In many countries curriculum history is now being systematically analysed and promoted. In the past few years educational journals in Brazil, Australia, Scandinavia and Spain have provided special editions on curriculum history,[20] and new books are planned in Germany, Portugal, Italy, South Africa and Japan.

Future directions for the study of the social construction of school curriculum will require a broadened approach. The base line of work reported above is only a precursor to more elaborate work. In particular this work will have to move into examining the relationship between school curriculum content and form, and issues of school practice, process and discourse. In addition, more broadly conceived notions of curriculum will have to be explored: the hidden curriculum, the curriculum conceived of as topics and activities and most important of all the primary and pre-school curriculum. As work begins to explore the way in which the school curriculum and its form and content relate to the parameters of practice, text and discourse, we shall begin to see in a more grounded way how the world of schooling is structured. To aid our theories further in this regard, more work must be undertaken on comparative studies of the school curriculum.

It is now vital in the United Kingdom to redirect this work to an exploration and critique of the National Curriculum (see Chapter 7), for the resonances at the level of class, gender and race to previous patterns are overwhelming. The National Curriculum cries out for the kind of social analysis first called for by Foster Watson;[21] to paraphrase, 'It is high time that the historical facts with regard to the National Curriculum were known, and known in connection with the social forces which brought them into the educational curriculum.' As I have detailed, work on the history of school subjects has been sustained, particularly in Britain itself, for over a decade of intensive scholarship. We now know a great deal about the socially constructed biases, selections and omissions embedded within school subjects. Yet in recent years, scholars close to these developments, with a few dignified exceptions, have virtually ignored this legacy in their work on the National Curriculum. The effect is to conspire with the Conservative governments' view that the National Curriculum is a new and compelling revolution in educational provision. In fact, curriculum history indicates that nothing could be further from the truth. As I have argued in Chapter 7, government policy and pronouncements have encouraged this amnesia and a failure to present academic challenges has the same effect.

Curriculum histories should provide a systematic analysis of the ongoing social constructions and selections that form the school curriculum, pointing up continuities and discontinuities of social purpose over time. It is important to note that not only is the prevailing paradigm of curriculum study focusing on implementation devoid of such socio-historical perspective, but more importantly so too is the more 'radical' focus on curriculum, which studies school-based 'resistance' to new national directives. Such work is not only without socio-historical range, it focuses only on the reaction. As Frederic Jameson recently noted in a conversation at the University of Western Ontario, 'The violence of the riposte says little about the terms of the engagement.' So it is with school resistance to the National Curriculum. The latter sets the terms of the engagement and does so in ways that links to a history of social purposes. Curriculum histories should seek to elucidate and analyse this ongoing process. They provide a new terrain of study where the school curriculum might again be employed as an entry point for social analysis.[22]

Developing a programme of work

Studies of the social construction of schooling and curriculum are now developing a sound and broad-based plateau of work from which new directions of study can be conceptualized and undertaken.

In recent work I have worked with and across the range of foci from the individual to the group and the collective.[23] In particular I have sought to examine individual life histories and how these allow us to develop themes and frameworks for viewing structures and organizations.[24] Some of the individual testimonies provided in this book show how teachers come to understand and reflect upon the broader contexts in which their professional lives are embedded. In one case, for instance, I conclude:

> in the life of Patrick Johnson we gain insights into him wrestling with imperatives in the social structure. From his early professional life he develops a vision of how schools might be, this vision is challenged and defeated as subject specialism and examinations invade the early secondary

modern schools; we see how one educational ideology is initially replaced by another as the teacher's career is constructed; the ideological renunciation only follows his retirement at the end of his career. Our attention is, therefore, left on the link between the structuring of material interests, strategies for career aggrandisement and the acceptance of particular educational ideologies.[25]

Likewise, I have tried to develop the group or collective focus by studying school subjects in historical evolution. Here I contended that

Historical case studies of school subjects provide the 'local detail' of curriculum change and conflict. The identification of individuals and subgroups actively at work within curriculum interest groups allows some examination and assessment of intention and motivation. Thereby sociological theories which attribute power over the curriculum to dominant interest groups can be scrutinised for their empirical potential.[26]

To concentrate attention at the meso-level of individual school subject groups is not to deny the crucial importance of macro-level economic changes or changes in intellectual ideas, dominant values or educational systems. But it is asserted that such macro-level changes may be actively reinterpreted at the meso-level. Changes at macro-level are viewed as presenting a range of new choices to subject factions, associations and communities. To understand how subjects change over time, as well as histories of intellectual ideas, we need to understand that subject groups are not all-powerful in engineering curriculum change but that their responses are a very important, and as yet neglected, part of the overall picture.

More recently I have been wrestling with how to integrate different foci and levels of analysis. In developing an integrated social constructionist perspective this work pursues the promise that the theoretical and the practical, or structure and agency, might be reconnected in our vision of curriculum scholarship. Were this to come about we might be saved from the recurrent 'flight to theory' followed by the counterbalancing 'flight to practice' (and the occasional intervening 'flight to the personal'). Our scholarship would thereby be encompassing in an integrated manner the complexity of levels of analysis that reflects the reality of curriculum.

To begin any analysis of schooling by accepting without question a form and content of curriculum that was fought for and achieved at a particular historical point on the basis of certain social and political priorities, to take that curriculum as a given, is to forgo a whole range of understandings and insights into features of the control and operation of the school and the classroom. It is to take over the mystifications of previous episodes of governance as unchallengeable givens. We have an arena of social production and reproduction – the school curriculum – where political and social priorities are paramount. Histories of other aspects of social life have begun systematically to scrutinize the process of social construction. Hobsbawn argues that the term 'invented tradition' 'includes both traditions actually invented, constructed and formally instituted and those emerging in a less traceable manner within a brief and dateable period – a matter of a few years perhaps – and establishing themselves with great rapidity.' Hobsbawn defines the matter this way:

> Invented tradition is taken to mean a set of practices, normally governed by overtly or tacitly accepted rules and of a ritual or symbolic nature which seek to circulate certain values and norms of behaviour by repetition, which automatically implies continuity with the past. In fact, where possible, they normally attempt to establish continuity with a suitable historic past.[27]

In this sense the making of curriculum can be seen as a process of inventing tradition. In fact this language is often used when the 'traditional disciplines' or 'traditional subjects' are juxtaposed against some new-fangled innovation of integrated or child-centred topics. The point, however, is that the written curriculum, whether as courses of study, syllabuses, guidelines or textbooks, is a supreme example of the invention of tradition; but as with all tradition it is not a once-and-for-all given, it is a given which has to be defended, where the mystifications have to be constructed and reconstructed over time. Plainly, if curriculum theorists substantially ignore the history and social construction of curriculum, such mystification and reproduction of 'traditional' curriculum form and content becomes easier.

An important stage, then, in the development of a social constructionist perspective is the production of a wide series of studies on the social construction of the prescriptive curriculum. But this is only a part of the story, as the advocates of 'practice' have long and correctly maintained. What is prescribed is not necessarily what is undertaken, and what is planned is not necessarily what happens. But, as we have argued, this should not imply that we abandon our studies of prescription as social construction and embrace, in singular form, the practical. We should instead seek to study the social construction of curriculum at the levels of both prescription and interaction.

The challenge is to develop new, substantive and methodological foci which integrate studies at the preactive and interactive levels. The linkage and integration of these studies is the major problem, for we are dealing with different levels and arenas of social construction. This difference of levels and arenas has often led to the argument that there is a complete break between preactive and interactive and that the latter is to all intents and purposes autonomous. This of course leads us back to the argument that 'practice is all that matters' and hence that we should focus our studies solely on practice.

The focus of recent curriculum study on projects and innovation (as noted earlier) is partly responsible for this belief in autonomy. Two observations from *Inside a Curriculum Project* illustrate this tendency: 'The project team had to explain what it was going to do before it could do it. The teachers started by doing it and only then looked for an explanation of why they were doing it that way.' But what was the 'it' the teachers were doing and how and where was it socially constructed. Likewise, 'the end product of the project was determined in the field, in contract with the school, not on the drawing board

. . . in the end it was what worked that survived.'[28] Both these observations celebrate the autonomy of the school and of practice. But both of them are likely to lead to our missing the point; for only what is prepared on the drawing board goes into the school and therefore *has a chance* to be interpreted and to survive. Of course, if this is so for the notoriously unloved curriculum project it is even more the case for the traditional (and less scrutinized and contested) school subject. With the latter, clear parameters to practice are socially constructed at the preactive level. Practice, in short, is socially constructed at the preactive *and* interactive levels: it is a combination of both and our curriculum study should acknowledge this combination.

If the questions of the form and scale of 'parameters' remain elusive, it is above all for this reason that we need to link our work on social construction at the preactive and interactive levels. At one level this will mean urging a closer connection between studies of school process and practice as currently constituted and analysis of discourses and studies of curriculum construction at the preactive level. A culminating stage in developing a social constructionist perspective would be to develop studies which themselves integrate studies of social construction at *both* preactive *and* interactive levels. We shall need to explore and develop integrative foci for social constructionist study and in this respect exploring the relational level would provide a strategy for strengthening and bringing together studies of action and of context in meaningful ways. Above all, social constructionist perspectives could improve our understanding of the politics of curriculum and in doing so would provide valuable 'cognitive maps' for teachers seeking to understand and locate the parameters to their practice. That would be their most valuable and continuing contribution at a time when state and bureaucratic prescriptions are becoming more and more invasive.

Notes and References

Critical Introduction

1. Schubert, W. H. (1993) Curriculum reform. In G. Cawelti (ed.) *Challenges and Achievements of American Education*, Alexandria, VA: Association for Supervision and Curriculum Development.
2. See, for example, Ball, S. J. and Bowe, R. (1992) Subject departments and the implementation of National Curriculum policy: an overview of the issues, *Journal of Curriculum Studies*, 24(2): 97–115. Similarly, a paper that explicitly sets out to articulate the relevance of the sociology of education for an analysis of the National Curriculum, oddly omits any substantial discussion of the most obvious part of the leverage and critique: that fundamental corpus of work (including Goodson's) on the history and politics of school subjects. What is represented is more a sociology of implementation and interpretation than one of hegemonic definition. The paper concerned is Halpin, D. (1990) The sociology of education and the National Curriculum, *British Journal of Sociology of Education*, 11(1): 21–35.
3. Pilger, J. (1992) *Distant Voices*, London: Vintage Press, p. 289.
4. Hargreaves, A. (1994) *Changing Teachers, Changing Times: Teachers' Work and Culture in the Postmodern Age*, London: Cassell; New York: Teachers' College Press; Toronto: OISE Press.
5. Bernstein, B. (1971) On the classification and framing of educational knowledge. In M. F. D. Young (ed.) *Knowledge and Control*, London: Collier-Macmillan, p. 47.
6. Young, M. F. D. (1971), op. cit., note 5.
7. Whitty, G. (1985) *Sociology and School Knowledge*, London: Methuen; Ball, S. and Lacey, C. (1980) Subject disciplines as the opportunity for group action. In P. Woods (ed.) *Teacher Strategies*, London: Croom Helm.
8. Hargreaves, A. and Earl, L. (1990) *Rights of Passage: a Review of Selected Research about Schooling in the Transition Years*, Toronto: Queen's Printer. This carries no guarantees, of course, that the reforms will be successful.
9. Woods, P. (1993) Managing marginality: teacher development through grounded life history, *British Educational Research Journal*, 19(4).
10. Hawking, S. (1988) *A Brief History of Time*, New York: Bantam Books.
11. See the obituary to J. Tuzo Wilson in Celebrated geologist, J. Tuzo Wilson, 84, *Toronto Star*, 17 April 1993: 16.

12. Chatwin, B. (1988) *The Songlines*, London: Picador, p. 17.
13. Hargreaves, A. (1994), op. cit.
14. Aronowitz, S. and Giroux, H. A. (1991) *Postmodern Education*, Minneapolis: University of Minnesota Press, p. 62.

Introduction

1. Goodson, I. F. and Anstead, C. (1993) *Through the Schoolhouse Door: Working Papers*, Toronto: Garamond Press.
2. Goodson, I. F. and Walker, R. (1991) *Biography, Identity and Schooling*, London, New York and Philadelphia: Falmer Press; Goodson, I. F. (ed.) (1992) *Studying Teachers' Lives*, London and New York: Routledge; Goodson, I. F. (forthcoming) *Representing Teachers*, London: Cassells and New York: Teachers College Press.
3. Goodson, I. F. and Dowbiggin, I. (1990) Docile bodies: commonalities in the history of psychiatry and schooling. In S. J. Ball (ed.) *Foucault and Education*, London and New York: Routledge, pp. 105–29.
4. The work of Caroline Gipps is exemplary in this regard, see Gipps, C. (1993) The profession of educational research, *British Educational Research Journal*, 19(1): 3–16; Gipps, C. (1990) The social implications of national assessment, *Urban Review*, 22(2): 145–59; Chitty, C. (1989) *Towards a New Education System: The Victory of the New Right*, London, New York and Philadelphia: Falmer Press; Jones, K. (1989) *Right Turn: The Conservative Revolution in Education*, London: Hutchinson Radius; Ball, S. J. (1990) *Politics and Policy Making in Education, Explorations in Policy Sociology*, London and New York: Routledge; Bowe, R. and Ball, S. J. with Gold, A. (1992) *Reforming Education and Changing Schools, Case Studies in Policy Sociology*, London and New York: Routledge; Edwards, G. (1992) A strategy for the curriculum: a response, *Journal of Curriculum Studies*, 24(5): 463–8; Graham, D. and Tytler, D. (1993) *A Lesson for Us All, The Making of the National Curriculum*, London and New York: Routledge.
5. Hargreaves, A. (1994) *Changing Teachers, Changing Times*, London: Cassells and New York: Teachers College Press.
6. Ahier, J. (1988) *Industry, Children and the Nation: an Analysis of National Identity in School Textbooks*, London, New York and Philadelphia: Falmer Press, p. 8.
7. Wexler, P. (1987) *Social Analysis of Education: After the New Sociology*, London: Routledge and Kegan Paul.
8. Goodson, I. F. and Anstead, C. (1993), op. cit.
9. McCulloch, G. (1993) Lessons from the Class of 1944? History as Education. An inaugural lecture delivered at The University of Lancaster on 17 February, p. 17.
10. Ibid., p. 23.

Chapter 1   Curriculum Reform and Curriculum Theory: A Case of Historical Amnesia

1. *Times Educational Supplement* (1987) 1904 and all that, *TES*, 31 July: 2.
2. Kliebard, H. (1986) *The Struggle for the American Curriculum 1893–1958*, London: Routledge and Kegan Paul, p. 269.
3. Goodson, I. F. (1988) *The Making of Curriculum – Collected Essays*, London, New York and Philadelphia: Falmer Press, p. 16.
4. Cox, C. B. and Dyson, A. E. (eds) (1969) *Fight for Education: a Black Paper*, London: The Critical Quarterly Society. Followed by Cox, C. B. and Boyson, R. (eds) (1975) *The Black Paper 1975*, London: Dent.

5. Her Majesty's Inspectorate (1979) *Aspects of Secondary Education*, London: HMSO.
6. Her Majesty's Inspectorate (1983) *9–13 Middle Schools – an Illustrative Survey*, London: HMSO.
7. Department of Education and Science (1983) *Teaching Quality*, London: HMSO, p. 19, para. 64 (i).
8. Ibid., p. 9, para. 29.
9. Ibid., p. 11, para. 37.
10. Ibid., para. 40.
11. Hargreaves, A. (1984) Curricular policy and the culture of teaching: some prospects for the future. Mimeo. See, for a later version, Chapter 4 of Hargreaves, A. (1989) *Curriculum and Assessment Reform*, Milton Keynes: Open University Press.
12. Department of Education and Science (1985) *Education 8 to 12 in Combined and Middle Schools: an HMI Survey*, London: HMSO.
13. Rowland, S. (1987) Where is primary education going? *Journal of Curriculum Studies*, 19(1): 90.
14. Hargreaves (1984), op. cit.
15. DES (1987) *The National Curriculum 5–16*, London: HMSO.
16. Wright Mills, C. (1970) *The Sociological Imagination*, Harmondsworth: Penguin, p. 165.
17. Feinberg, W. (1983) *Understanding Education: Towards a Reconstruction of Educational Enquiry*, Cambridge: Cambridge University Press, p. 86.
18. Ibid. See Goodson (1988), op. cit., pp. 62–3.
19. Esland, G. M. (1971) Teaching and learning as the organisation of knowledge. In M. F. D. Young (ed.) *Knowledge and Control: New Directions for the Sociology of Education*, London: Collier Macmillan, p. 111.

Chapter 2   On Understanding Curriculum: The Alienation of Curriculum Theory

1. *Concise Oxford Dictionary* (1964) Oxford: Oxford University Press.
2. Reid, W. A. (1978) *Thinking About the Curriculum*, London: Routledge & Kegan Paul, p. 17.
3. Wise, A. E. (1979) *Legislated Learning: the Bureaucratization of the American Classroom*, Berkeley: University of California Press, pp. 54–5.
4. Wirth, A. G. (1983) *Productive Work in Industry and Schools*, New York: University Press of America, p. 120.
5. Wise (1979), op. cit., p. 94.
6. Kliebard, H. (1975) Persistent curriculum issues in historical perspective. In W. Pinar (ed.) *Curriculum Theorizing*, Berkeley, CA: McCutchan, p. 41.
7. Westbury, I. (1973) Conventional classrooms, 'open' classrooms and the technology of teaching, *Journal of Curriculum Studies*, 5(2): 99.
8. Segal, C. (1984) *The Observer*, 17 June.
9. Reid, W. A. (1978) *Thinking About the Curriculum*, London: Routledge & Kegan Paul p. 10.
10. Hirst, P. M. (1965) Liberal education and the nature of knowledge. In R. D. Archambault (ed.) *Philosophical Analysis and Education*, London: Routledge & Kegan Paul, p. 127.
11. Pring, R. (1972) Focus of knowledge and general education, *General Education*, 19: 27.
12. Phenix, P. M. (1968) The disciplines as curriculum content. In E. C. Short and C. D. Marconnit (eds) *Contemporary Thought on Public School Curriculum: Readings*, Dubuque, Iowa: W. C. Brown Co., p. 133.

13. Lawton, D. (1975) *Class, Culture and the Curriculum*, London: Routledge & Kegan Paul, p. 18.
14. Ibid., p. 85.
15. Hirst, P. M. (1974) *Knowledge and the Curriculum*, London: Routledge & Kegan Paul, p. 99.
16. Goodlad, I. (1975) A perspective on accountability, *Phi Delta Kappa*, 57(2 October): 10.
17. House, E. (1978) Evaluation as scientific management in US school reform, *Comparative Education Review*, 22(3): 400.
18. Berger, P. L. and Luckman, T. (1967) *The Social Construction of Reality*, Harmondsworth: Allen Lane.
19. Schwab, J. L. (1978) *Science, Curriculum and Liberal Education* (edited by I. Westbury and N. Wilkof), Chicago: University of Chicago Press, p. 287.
20. Ibid.
21. Stenhouse, L. (1975) *An Introduction to Curriculum Research and Development*, London: Heinemann, pp. 24–5.
22. Walker, R. (1974) *Classroom Research: a View of SAFARI. Innovation, Evaluation, Research and the Problem of Control*, Norwich: CARE, p. 22.
23. Barton, L. and Lawn, M. (1980/1) Back inside the whole: a curriculum case study, *Interchange*, 11(4): 4.
24. This critique refers to CARE in the 1970s. The subsequent work at the Centre has moved to develop a range of important theoretical traditions and has stood as an important counterpoint to some of the simplifications of New Right policies.
25. Macdonald, B. (1976) Who's afraid of education? *Education 3–13*, 14(2): 89.
26. Hoyle, E. (1969) How does the curriculum change? A proposal for inquiries, *Journal of Curriculum Studies*, 1: 2.
27. Parlett, M. and Hamilton, D. (1972) *Evaluation as Illumination, Occasional Paper 9*, Edinburgh: Centre for Research in Educational Sciences.
28. Sylvester, D. (1973) *History 13–16*, London: Schools Council, p. 144.
29. Goodson, I. F. (1980) History 13–16. In L. Stenhouse (ed.) *Curriculum Research and Development in Action*, London: Heinemann, p. 187.
30. Curriculum Development Unit (1982) *Educational Achievement and Youth Employment*, Dublin: Trinity College, p. 71.
31. Ibid.
32. McKinney, W. L. and Westbury, I. (1975) Stability and change: the public school of Gary, Indiana, 1940–70. In W. A. Reid and D. F. Walker (eds) *Case Studies in Curriculum Change*, London: Routledge and Kegan Paul, p. 6.
33. This aspect has recently been explored in Haft, H. and Hopmann, S. (eds) (1990) *Case Studies in Curriculum Administration History*, London, New York and Philadelphia: Falmer. See also Apple, M. W. (1990) *Ideology and Curriculum*, 2nd edn, London and New York: Routledge.

Chapter 3   Curriculum History, Professionalization and the Social Organization of Knowledge

1. For instance, see volume 17 (1988) of the *History of Education Review*, particularly the articles by P. W. Musgrave, David Layton and Gary McCulloch.
2. For an account of recent historiographic trends in education, see Gaffield, C. (1986) Coherence and chaos in educational historiography, *Interchange*, 17: 112–21.

3. We use Bucher and Strauss's definition of professions 'as loose amalgamations of segments pursuing different manners and more or less delicately held together under a common name at a particular period in history'. Bucher, R. and Strauss, A. (1961) Professions in process, *American Journal of Sociology*, 66: 325–34.

4. For recent accounts of the theory of cultural hegemony and its relevance to the history and sociology of education, see Connell, *et al.* (1983) *Making the Difference.* Sydney: George Allen and Unwin; Connell, R. W. (1988) Curriculum politics, hegemony, and strategies of social change, *Curriculum and Teaching*, 3: 63–71; Giroux, H. (1983) Theories of reproduction and resistance in the new sociology of education: a critical analysis, *Harvard Educational Review*, 53: 257–93; Labaree, D. F. (1986) Curriculum, credentials, and the middle class: a case study of a nineteenth-century high school, *Sociology of Education*, 59: 42–57. See also Lears, T. J. J. (1986) The concept of cultural hegemony: problems and possibilities, *American Historical Review*, 90: 567–93.

5. One of the chief advantages of a different agenda grounded in curriculum history is that it links the history of education with equally innovative developments in the social history of knowledge, a field that, thanks to the insights of scholars such as Karl Mannheim, Michael Foucault, Pierre Bourdieu, Michael Young, Basil Bernstein and Christopher Lasch, is making progress towards an understanding of the relationship between the historical construction of knowledge by professionals and the discipline, classification and control of vulnerable social groups. For example, see Mannheim, K. (1972) *Ideology and Utopia: an Introduction to the Sociology of Knowledge*, London: Routledge and Kegan Paul; Foucault, M. (1979) *Discipline and Punish: the Birth of the Prison* (trans. Alan Sheridan), New York: Vintage; Bourdieu, P. and Passeron, J. C. (1977) *Reproduction in Education, Society, and Culture*, Beverly Hills, CA: Sage; Young, M. F. D. (1971) Approach to the study of curricula as socially organized knowledge. In M. F. D. Young (ed.) *Knowledge and Control: New Directions for the Sociology of Education*, London: Collier-Macmillan; Bernstein, B. (1977) *Class, Codes, and Controls*, 3 vols, London: Routledge and Kegan Paul; Lasch, C. (1978) *The Culture of Narcissism: American Life in an Age of Diminishing Expectations*, New York: Norton. We shall explore the implications of professional knowledge for client populations in more detail in an upcoming paper.

6. Layton, D. (1973) *Science for the People*, London: George Allen and Unwin; Waring, M. (1979) *Social Pressures and Curriculum Innovation: a Study of the Nuffield Foundation Science Teaching Project*, London: Methuen; Silver, H. (1983) *Education as History*, New York: Methuen. See also the excellent study by Hamilton, D. (1989) *Towards a Theory of Schooling*, London, New York and Philadelphia: Falmer.

7. See Goodson, I. F. (1993) *School Subjects and Curriculum Change*, London, New York and Philadelphia: Falmer; (1988) *The Making of Curriculum: Collected Essays*, London, New York and Philadelphia: Falmer. A much more detailed analysis of the history of school science is contained in Goodson, I. F. and Marsh, C. (forthcoming) *Studying School Subjects*, London, New York and Philadelphia: Falmer.

8. Tracey, C. W. (1962) Biology: its struggle for recognition in English schools during the period 1900–60, *School Science Review*, 93: 423.

9. Ministry of Education (1960) *Science in Secondary Schools*, Ministry of Education Pamphlet No. 38, London: HMSO.

10. Layton, D. (1973), op. cit., p. 41.

11. Wrottesley, Lord J. (1860) *Thoughts on Government and Legislation*, London: John Murray. Cited in Hodson, D. (1987) Science curriculum change in Victorian

England: a case study of the science of common things. In I. F. Goodson (ed.) *International Perspectives in Curriculum History*, London: Croom Helm, p. 36.

12. Woolnough, B. (1988) *Physics Teaching in Schools, 1960–1985*, London, New York and Philadelphia: Falmer.

13. Tomkins, G. (1986) *A Common Countenance*, Scarborough, Ont.: Prentice Hall, pp. 82–3.

14. Gingras, Y. (1986) The institutionalization of scientific research in Canadian universities: the case of physics, *Canadian Historical Review*, 67: 182–3.

15. Reid, W. A. (1984) Curricular topics as institutional categories: implications for theory and research in the history and sociology of school subjects. In I. F. Goodson and S. J. Ball (eds) *Defining the Curriculum: Histories and Ethnographies*, Lewes: Falmer, pp. 67–75. See also Meyer, J. W. (1978) The structure of educational organization. In J. W. Meyer and W. Marshall *et al.* (eds) *Environments and Organizations*, San Francisco: Jossey Bass; (1980) Levels of the educational system and schooling effects. In C. E. Bidwell and D. M. Windham (eds) *The Analysis of Educational Productivity*, 2 vols, Cambridge, MA: Ballinger.

16. Thackray, A. (1974) Natural knowledge in cultural context: the Manchester model, *American Historical Review*, 79: 675, 678, 679, 682, 686, 693, 698. See also Berman, M. (1978) *Social Change and Scientific Organization: the Royal Institution, 1799–1844*, Ithaca, NY: Cornell University Press; for a qualification of the Thackray thesis, see Inkster, I. (1982) Variations on a theme by Thackray: comments on provincial science, culture, ca. 1780–1850, *British Society for the History of Science Newsletter*, 8: 15–18. A useful discussion of this general issue within the context of Anglo-American medicine in the nineteenth century is in Shortt, S. E. D. (1983) Physicians, science, and status: issues in the professionalization of Anglo-American medicine in the nineteenth century, *Medical History*, 27: 51–68. For the most extensive treatment of this issue in the history of medicine, see Ackerknecht, E. H. (1973) *Therapeutics: from the Primitives to the Twentieth Century*, New York, Hafner, passim. For a more specific case study of this discrepancy between medical theory and therapeutics and the way scientific knowledge could be exploited by groups seeking professional objectives, see Brown, T. M. (1970) The college of physicians and the acceptance of iatromechanism in England, 1665–1695, *Bulletin of the History of Medicine*, 44: 12–30. The pioneering study of discontinuity in the history of scientific ideas is Kuhn, T. S. (1962) *The Structure of Scientific Revolutions*, Chicago: University of Chicago Press. A thoughtful attempt to exploit Kuhn's insights as a way of pursuing an 'externalist' approach to the history of science and medicine is Brown, T. M. (1980) Putting paradigms into history, *Marxist Perspectives*, 34–63.

17. In fact, one of the earliest modern asylums in Britain was named the York Retreat. See Digby, A. (1986) Moral treatment at the retreat, 1796–1846. In W. F. Bynum, R. Porter, and M. Shepherd (eds) *The Anatomy of Madness: Essays in the History of Psychiatry, Volume Two: Institutions and Society*, London and New York: Tavistock, pp. 52–72.

18. There is now a considerable literature on the growth of public and private asylums in France and the Anglo-American world in the nineteenth century. The most important contributions are Rothman, D. (1971) *The Discovery of the Asylum: Social Order and Disorder in the New Republic*, Boston and Toronto: Little, Brown; Scull, A. T. (1979) *Museums of Madness: the Social Organization of Insanity in Ninetenth-century England*. Harmondsworth: Penguin: Grob, G. N. (1973) *Mental Institutions in America: Social Policy to 1875*, New York: Free Press; Castel, R. (1976) *L'ordre psychiatrique: L'age d'or de l'alienisme*, Paris: Editions de Minuit; Tomes, N. (1985) *A*

Generous Confidence: Thomas Story Kirkbride and the Art of Asylum-keeping, 1840–1883, New York: Cambridge University Press; Shortt, S. E. D. (1986) *Victorian Lunacy: Richard M. Bucke and the Practice of Late Nineteenth-century Psychiatry*, New York: Cambridge University Press; Goldstein, J. (1987) *Console and Classify: the French Psychiatric Profession in the Nineteenth Century*, New York: Cambridge University Press. The pioneering work in revisionist theory regarding the birth of the asylum is Foucault, M. (1973) *Madness and Civilization: a History of Insanity in the Age of Reason* (trans. R. Howard), New York: Vintage. Some collections of essays in the history of psychiatry deal with the topic of the birth of the asylum. See for example, Scull, A. T. (ed.) (1981) *Madhouses, Mad-doctors, and Madmen: the Social History of Psychiatry in the Victorian Era*, Philadelphia: University of Pennsylvania Press; Bynum, W. F., Porter, R. and Shepherd, M. (eds) (1985) *The Anatomy of Madness: Essays in the History of Psychiatry*, 2 vols, London: Tavistock.

19. For the clearest expression of the professional objectives of late nineteenth-century French psychiatry, see Lunier, C. and Dumesnil (1878) *Rapport general a M. le Ministre de l'Interieur sur le service des alienes en 1874*, Paris: Imprimerie nationale.

20. For an account of the eventual victory of the clinical, somatic, and pathological orientation in England, see Clark, M. J. (1981) The rejection of psychological approaches to mental disorder in late nineteenth-century British psychiatry. In Scull, A. (ed.) (1981), op. cit., pp. 271–312. The struggle between psychoanalysis and the biomedical model in American psychiatry and neurology in the early twentieth century is one of the topics Hale, N. G. (1971) has dealt with in *Freud and the Americans: the Beginnings of Psychoanalysis in the United States, 1876–1917*, New York: Oxford University Press.

21. Friedson, E. (1970) *Professional Dominance*, New York: Atherton, p. 106.

22. Historical interest in degeneracy theory has been growing recently. See, for example Dowbiggin, I. R. (1985) Degeneration and hereditarianism in French mental medicine, 1840–1900. In Bynum, Porter, and Shepherd (eds) (1985), op. cit., vol. 1, pp. 188–232; Shortt (1986), op. cit., pp. 100–9. See also Nye, R. A. (1984) *Crime, Madness, and Politics in Modern France: the Medical Concept of National Decline*, Princeton, NJ: Princeton University Press, *passim*.

23. For examples of this attitude, see Ball, B. (1880) La medecine a travers les siecles, *Annales medico-psychologiques*, 3: 28; Camuset, L. (1882) Revue de J. Luys, *Traite clinique et pratique des maladies mentales*, *Annales medico-psychologiques*, 7: 509.

24. For the influence of positivism on republican politicians, see Elwitt, S. (1975) *The Making of the Third Republic: Class and Politics in France, 1868–1884*, Baton Rouge: Louisiana State University Press, esp. pp. 170–229. See also Keylor, W. R. (1981) Anticlericalism and educational reform in the French third republic: a retrospective evaluation, *History of Education Quarterly*, 21: 95–103. For an account of the dramatic changes within science faculties in late nineteenth-century France, see Fox, R. (1984) Science, the university, and the state in nineteenth-century France. In G. L. Geison (ed.) *Professions and the French State, 1700–1900*, Philadelphia: University of Pennsylvania Press, pp. 66–145.

25. Weisz, G. (1980) Reform and conflict in French medical education, 1870–1914. In R. Fox and G. Weisz (eds) *The Organization of Science and Technology in France, 1808–1914*, Cambridge: Cambridge University Press, p. 65.

26. To use Eliot Friedson's words, prospective psychiatrists could now receive instruction in 'a curriculum that includes some special theoretical content', which 'may represent a declaration that there is a body of special knowledge and skill necessary for the occupation' of psychiatry. Friedson (1970), op. cit., pp. 134–5.

27. Kaestle, C. F. (1972) Social reform and the urban school, *History of Education Quarterly*, 12: 218.
28. Weber, M. (1958) Bureaucracy. In H. Gerth and C. W. Mills (eds) *From Max Weber*, Oxford: Oxford University Press, pp. 240, 243. Cited in Redner, H. (1987) The institutionalization of science: a critical synthesis, *Social Epistemology*, 1: 37–59. We do not mean to suggest that the content of knowledge is inconsequential at any time in the social history of knowledge. We mean only that the explicitly instrumental application of bodies of knowledge diminishes in inverse relation to the seriousness and success of professional attempts to improve their material conditions.

Chapter 4   Behind the Schoolhouse Door: The Historical Study of the Curriculum

1. Society for the Study of Curriculum History (1981) Papers of the Society for the Study of Curriculum History. Pennsylvania State University, p. 1.
2. Webster, J. R. (1976) Curriculum change and 'crisis', *British Journal of Educational Studies*, 24(3): 206–7.
3. Waring, M. (1975) *Aspects of the dynamics of curriculum reform in secondary school science*, PhD thesis, University of London.
4. Charlton, K. (1968) The contribution of history to the study of curriculum. In J. F. Kerr (ed.) *Changing the Curriculum*, London: University of London Press, pp. 70–1.
5. Blumer, H. (1969) *Symbolic Interactionism: Perspective and Method*, Englewood Cliffs, NJ: Prentice Hall, p. 60.
6. Stenhouse, L. (1976) *Case study as a basis for research in a theoretical contemporary history of education*. Mimeo, p. 7.
7. Williamson, B. (1974) Continuities and discontinuities in the sociology of education. In M. Flude and J. Ahier (eds) *Educability, Schools and Ideology*, London: Croom Helm, p. 10.
8. See Goodson, I. F. (1988) *The Making of Curriculum: Collected Essays*, London, New York and Philadelphia: Falmer.
9. Judd, C. M. (1914) *The Training of Teachers in England, Scotland and Germany*, Washington, DC: Bureau of Education.
10. Fiorino, A. (1978) *Teacher Education in Ontario: a History, 1843–1976*, Ontario: Commission on Declining School Enrolments in Ontario; Altenbaugh, R. J. and Underwood, K. (1990) The evolution of the normal school. In J. I. Goodlad, R. Soder and K. A. Sirotnik (eds) *Places Where Teachers Are Taught*, San Francisco: Jossey-Bass, pp. 136–86; Beatty, B. (1990) Teaching teachers in private universities. In J. I. Goodlad, R. Soder and K. A. Sirotnik (eds) *Places Where Teachers Are Taught*, San Francisco: Jossey-Bass.
11. Cremin, L., Shannon, D. A. and Townsend, M. E. (1954) *A History of Teachers College, Columbia University*, New York: Columbia University Press; Herbst, J. (1989) *And Sadly Teach: Teacher Education and Professionalization in American Culture*, Madison: University of Wisconsin Press.
12. Cremin, Shannon and Townsend (1954), op. cit., p. 42.
13. Seaborne, M. (1971) The history of education. In J. W. Tibble (ed.) *An Introduction to the Study of Education*, London: Routledge and Kegan Paul, pp. 65–79.
14. Cohen, S. (1976) The history of the history of American Education, 1900–1976: the uses of the past, *Harvard Educational Review*, 46: 298–330; Cohen, S. (1984) Reconstructing the history of urban education in America. In G. Grace (ed.)

Education and the City: Theory, History and Contemporary Practice, Boston: Routledge and Kegan Paul, pp. 115–38; Weiner, L. (1991) Teachers: lost at the crossroads of historiography, Paper presented at the AERA Annual Meeting, Chicago, April.

15. Davis, R. H. C. (1981) The content of history, *History*, 66(218): 361–74.
16. Higham, J. (1965) *History: Professional Scholarship in America*, New York: Prentice-Hall; Berger, C. (1986) *The Writing of Canadian History*, 2nd edn, Toronto: University of Toronto Press.
17. Williams, R. (1961) *The Long Revolution*, Harmondsworth: Penguin, p. 67.
18. Andrews, A. (1983) In pursuit of the past: some problems in the collection, analysis and use of historical documentary evidence. Paper delivered at Whitelands College Workshop, 'Qualitative Methodology and the Study of Education'.
19. For an earlier – and harsher – generation of such criticism, see Bester, A. (1953) *Educational Wastelands*, Urbana: University of Illinois Press; Bailyn, B. (1960) *Education in the Forming of American Society: Needs and Opportunities for Study*, Chapel Hill: University of North Carolina Press.
20. Gaffield, C. (1986) Back to school: towards a new agenda for the history of education, *Acadiensis*, 15(2): 183, 187–8.
21. Silver, H. (1992) Knowing and not knowing in the history of education, *History of Education*, 21(1): 104.
22. Ibid., p. 107.
23. Simon, B. (1966) The history of education. In J. W. Tibble (ed.) *The Study of Education*, London: Routledge and Kegan Paul, 91–131.
24. Watson, F. (1909) *The Beginnings of the Teaching of Modern Subjects in England*, London: Pitman, p. viii.
25. Hobsbawm, E. J. (1959) *Primitive Rebels*, reprinted New York: Norton, 1965; Thompson, E. P. (1968) *The Making of the English Working Class*, Harmondsworth, Penguin; Genovese, E. D. (1974) *Roll, Jordan, Roll: the World the Slaves Made*, New York: Random House; Smith-Rosenberg, C. (1985) *Disorderly Conduct*, Oxford: Oxford University Press.
26. Wilson, J. D. (1984) From social control to family strategies: some observations on recent trends in Canadian educational history, *History of Education Review*, 13(1): 1–13; (1990) The new diversity in Canadian educational history, *Acadiensis* 19(2): 148–69; Gaffield (1986), op. cit.; Harrigan, P. J. (1986) A comparative perspective on recent trends in the history of education in Canada, *History of Education Quarterly*, 26(1): 71–86; Aldrich, R. (1987) Central issues in history of education: an English perspective, *Canadian History of Education Association Bulletin*, 4(3): 17–25.
27. Wilson (1984), op. cit.
28. Waring, M. (1979) *Social Pressures and Curriculum Innovation: a Study of the Nuffield Foundation Science Teaching Project*, London: Methuen; Silver, H. (1983) *Education as History: Interpreting Nineteenth and Twentieh Century Education*, London: Methuen; Labaree, D. (1988) *The Making of an American High School: the Credentials Market and the Central High School of Philadelphia, 1838–1939*, New Haven, CT: Yale University Press; Rowell, P. M. and Gaskell, P. J. (1987) Tensions and realignments: school physics in British Columbia 1955–1980. In I. F. Goodson (ed.) *International Perspectives in Curriculum History*, London: Croom Helm, 74–106.
29. Cuban, L. (1984) *How Teachers Taught: Constancy and Change in American Classrooms, 1890–1980*, New York: Longman; Prentice, A. and Theobald, M. (eds) (1991) *Women Who Taught: Perspectives on the History of Women and Teaching*, Toronto: University of Toronto Press (this work should be read alongside Jane Bernard Powers' (1990) splendid study *The 'Girl Question' in Education: Vocational*

Training for Young Women in the Progressive Era, London, New York and Philadelphia: Falmer Press); Goodson, I. F. (ed.) (1992) *Studying Teachers' Lives*, London: Routledge. These studies also build on the work of those researching more contemporary issues. See especially Connelly, F. M. and Clandinin, D. J. (1988) *Teachers as Curriculum Planners: Narrative of Experience*, New York: Teachers College Press.

30. Tyack, D., Lowe, R. and Hansot, E. (1984) Behind the schoolhouse door. Chapter 4 in *Public Schools in Hard Times: The Great Depression and Recent Years*. Cambridge, MA: Harvard University Press; Sutherland, N. (1986) The triumph of 'Formalism': elementary schooling in Vancouver from the 1920s to the 1960s. In R. A. J. McDonald and Jean Barman (eds) *Vancouver Past: Essays in Social History*, Vancouver: University of British Columbia Press, pp. 175–210.

31. Andrews (1983), op. cit.

32. On history and postmodernism, see Buhle, M. J. and Buhle, P. (1988) The new labor history at the cultural crossroads, *Journal of American History*, 75(1), 151–7; Ankersmit, F. R. (1989) Historiography and postmodernism, *History and Theory*, 28(2): 137–53; Harlan, D. (1989) Intellectual history and the return of literature, *American Historical Review*, 94(3): 581–609.

33. Waring (1975), op. cit., p. 12.

34. Wineburg, S. S. (1991) On the reading of historical texts: Notes on the breach between school and academy, *American Educational Research Journal*, 28(3): 495–519.

35. The use of arguments from the postmodern movement in literary criticism has brought this emphasis on the historian's subjective role in creating an interpretation of the past to the fore in historical debate.

Chapter 5 Vocational Education and School Reform: The Case of the London (Canada) Technical School, 1900–1930

1. For accounts of Canadian vocational education that reach this conclusion, see Morrison, T. R. (1974) Reform as social tracking: the case of industrial education in Ontario, 1870–1900, *Journal of Educational Thought*, 8: 76–110; Lazerson, M. and Dunn, T. A. (1977) Schools and the work crisis: vocationalism in Canadian education. In H. A. Stevenson and J. D. Wilson (eds) *Precepts, Policy, and Process: Perspectives on Contemporary Canadian Education*, London, Ontario: Alexander, Blake Associates pp. 285–304; Dunn, T. A. (1979) Teaching the meaning of work: vocational education in British Columbia, 1900–1929. In Jones, D. C., Sheehan, N. M. and Stamp, R. M. (eds) *Shaping the Schools of the Canadian West*, Calgary: Detselig Enterprises pp. 236–55; (1980) Vocationalism and its promoters in British Columbia, 1900–1929, *Journal of Educational Thought*, 14: 91–107; Crowley, T. (1986) Madonnas before Magdelenes: Adelaide Hoodless and the making of the Canadian Gibson Girl, *Canadian Historical Review*, 68: 520–47; Jackson, N. S. and Gaskell, J. S. (1987) White collar vocationalism: the rise of commercial education in Ontario and British Columbia, 1870–1920, *Curriculum Inquiry*, 17: 177–210. For alternative interpretations of vocational education in Canada, see Stamp, R. M. (1970) The campaign for technical education in Ontario, 1876–1914, PhD, London, Ont.: University of Western Ontario; (1976) Technical education, the national policy, and federal-provincial relations in education, 1899–1919, *Canadian Historical Review*, 52: 404–23; Pederson, D. (1983) The scientific training of mothers: the campaign for domestic science in Ontario schools, 1890–1913. In

R. A. Jarrell and A. E. Ross (eds) *Critical Issues in the History of Canadian Science, Technology, and Medicine*, Thornhill, Ont.: HSTC Publications pp. 178–94. For critical interpretations of US vocational education, see Lazerson, M. and Norton Grubb, W. (eds) (1974) *American Education and Vocationalism: A Documentary History, 1870–1970*, New York: Teachers College Press; Kantor, H. A. and Tyack, D. (eds) (1982) *Work, Youth, and Schooling*, Stanford: Stanford University Press; Hogan, D. J. (1985) *Class and Reform: School and Society in Chicago, 1880–1930*, Philadelphia: University of Pennsylvania Press, pp. 138–93; Kantor, H. A. (1988) *Learning to Earn: School, Work, and Vocational Reform in California, 1880–1930*, Madison: University of Wisconsin Press. Two recent publications which document the shortcomings of contemporary vocational education are Radwanski, G. (1987) *The Ontario Study of the Relevance of Education and the Issue of Dropouts*, Toronto: Ministry of Education; and William T. Grant Foundation Commission on Work, Family, and Citizenship (1988) *The Forgotten Half: Non-College Youth in America. An Interim Report on the School-to-Work Transition*, Washington, DC: The Commission.

2. For an excellent treatment of the historical relationship between curriculum and credentials, see Labaree, D. F. (1988) *The Making of an American High School: The Credentials Market and the Central High School of Philadelphia, 1838–1939*, New Haven and London: Yale University Press.

3. One example of United States resistance to the notion that vocational schooling was an equal partner of academic schooling in public education was the conflict over the Cooley Bill in Illinois during the second decade of the twentieth century. See Hogan (1985), op. cit., pp. 175–81.

4. For two recent accounts of the history of 'social efficiency' theory in education, see Kliebard, H. M. (1986) *The Struggle for the American Curriculum, 1893–1958*, Boston and London: Routledge and Kegan Paul, and Henley: pp. 89–122 and 123–52; Franklin, B. M. (1986) *Building the American Community: The School Curriculum and the Search for Social Control*, London, New York and Philadelphia: Falmer Press: especially pp. 83–118.

5. Palmer, B. D. (1979) *A Culture in Conflict: Skilled Workers and Industrial Capitalism in Hamilton, Ontario, 1860–1914*, Montreal: McGill-Queen's University Press; (1983) *Working-Class Experience: The Rise and Reconstitution of Canadian Labour, 1800–1980*, Toronto: Butterworths. See also Kealey, G. S. and Warrian, P. (eds) (1976) *Essays in Canadian Working Class History*, Toronto: McClelland and Stewart; Kealey, G. S. (ed.) (1973) *Canada Investigates Industrialism: The Royal Commission on the Relations of Labour and Capital 1889*, Toronto: University of Toronto Press; Brown, R. C. and Cook, R. (1974) *Canada, 1896–1921: A Nation Transformed*, Toronto: McClelland and Stewart: pp. 108–26. The best summary of developments in commercial work in Ontario is Jackson and Gaskell (1987), op. cit.

6. Heron, C. and Palmer, B. D. (1977) Through the prism of the strike: industrial conflict in Southern Ontario, 1901–1914, *Canadian Historical Review*, 58: 421–58; Palmer, B. D. (1976) 'Give us the road and we will run it': the social and cultural matrix of an emerging labour movement. In Kealey and Warrian (1976), op. cit., pp. 106–24.

7. Canada (1889) *Report of the Royal Commission on the Relations of Capital and Labour in Canada, Ontario Evidence*, Ottawa: 587–9, 599, 604–5 and 669–70.

8. Canada (1913) *Report of the Royal Commission on Industrial Training and Technical Education*, Parts I–IV, Ottawa: C. H. Parmalee, part IV, pp. 2084–2113. For other testimony of the business community in Ontario, see Seath, J. (1911) *Education for Industrial Purposes*, Toronto: L. K. Cameron: pp. 351–75.

9. See Archer, M. (1979) *Social Origins of Educational Systems*. Beverly Hills, CA: Sage, pp. 53–214. See also Rubinson, R. (1986) Class formation, politics, and institutions: schooling in the United States, *American Journal of Sociology*, 92: 519–48, esp. 526.

10. Ringer, R. (1987) Introduction. In D. K. Muller, F. Ringer and B. Simon (eds) *The Rise of the Modern Educational System: Structural Change and Social Reproduction, 1870–1920*, Cambridge: Cambridge University Press: p. 8.

11. One tactic vocational reformers employed was to minimize over time the distinctions between the curricula of technical schools and academic high schools by stressing the part of the vocational curriculum devoted to academic subjects. For similar developments in France in the nineteenth century, see Fritz Ringer F. (1987) On segmentation in modern European education systems: the case of French secondary education, 1865–1920. In Muller, Ringer and Simon (1987), op. cit., p. 62.

12. Trades and Labour Council of Canada (1910) *Proceedings*, pp. 47–58.

13. Ontario Legislative Assembly (1911) *Statutes of the Province of Ontario*, Toronto, An Act Respecting Education for Industrial Purposes, pp. 525–30.

14. *London Free Press (FP)* (1901), 2 May.

15. For accounts of London's social and industrial nature, see Palmer (1976), op. cit., pp. 107–10 and 426–7; see also *London and Its Men of Affairs*, London, n.d., pp. 126–47. For data on London see Department of Trade and Commerce (1921) *Census of Canada*, Ottawa: vol. 4, pp. 420–39, vol. 3, p. 240; and (1931) vol. 7, pp. 276–87, 748–51.

16. London Chamber of Commerce, Minutes of the London Board of Trade, Box 5527, p. 393, Weldon Library, University of Western Ontario (WL, U of WO). See also the memorandum of Fitzgerald, W. C. (1907) Chairman of the London Board of Education, *Minutes of the London Board of Education* (London, *Minutes*), pp. 216–17.

17. One episode which demonstrated the ambivalence of organized labour towards technical education was the 19 October 1910 meeting of the London chapter of the TLC. At this meeting it was carried that local chapters of the TLC be encouraged to notify the Royal Commission on Industrial Training and Technical Education that they were in favour of technical education but not manual training. London, TLC minutes and records, 19 October 1910, box 5612, WL U of WO. See also *FP* 18 October, 19 October 1910 for the comments of London TLC members to Royal Commission.

18. *Industrial Banner (IB)* (1919), 26 September.

19. Beal's intellectual debt to the theory of 'social efficiency' can be seen in his President's address, Ontario Educational Association (1928) *Proceedings*, pp. 125–30.

20. *FP* (1912), 7 November.

21. *FP* (1910), 19 October.

22. Armstrong, F. H. (1986) *The Forest City: An illustrated History of London, Canada*, Northridge, California: Windsor Publications, p. 165.

23. See Seath (1911), op. cit. See also Semple, S. (1964) John Seath's concept of vocational education in the school system of Ontario, 1884–1911, MEd thesis, Toronto: University of Toronto; Brewin, M. J. (1967) The establishment of an industrial education system in Ontario, MEd thesis, Toronto: Ontario Institute for Studies in Education; Stamp (1970), op. cit., pp. 255–6.

24. London Board of Education (1912) *Annual Report of the London Board of Education (ARL)*, pp. 24–38.

25. Ontario, Department of Education (1917) *Annual Report of the Minister of Education (ARM)*, Toronto, pp. 37–8. For a typical characterization of the theory of administrative 'efficiency' in Ontario education in the early twentieth century, see Toronto Board of Education (1915) *Annual Report of the Toronto Board of Education*, Toronto, p. 42. Cited in Corrigan, P. and Curtis, B. (1985) Education, inspection, and state formation: a preliminary statement, *Canadian Historical Association Papers*, p. 170.
26. *ARM* (1916), p. 61.
27. London (1913) *Minutes*, pp. 194–95.
28. *London Advertiser (LA)* (1918), 29 August.
29. *LA*, 28 January 1914. Merchant's dissatisfaction with the accommodation for technical day classes was not his only complaint. He was also displeased that day school attendance for boys at the London Industrial School had actually decreased since his visit in 1913. Why he should have felt this way is not altogether clear. However, if Jackson and Gaskell (op. cit., p. 191) are correct that teachers in Ontario believed females constituted 'a less prestigious student clientele' in the early twentieth century, then it is plausible that Merchant sought higher enrolment figures for males at the day school because he wished to improve the status of technical education. From the data for evening class enrolment in London by gender for each subject, it seems that the London Industrial School was a largely female institution, and Merchant may have felt that the presence of more boys would undermine this early image of the school. For confirmation of Merchant's dissatisfaction, see London, *Minutes*, 1915, p. 158. For a sample of enrolment figures for night school subjects in London, see *ARM* (1913), pp. 820–1.
30. *ARM* (1916), p. 61.
31. London (1915) *Minutes*, pp. 49–53.
32. London (1916) *Minutes*, pp. 11–14, 32–7.
33. *FP*, 19 November 1913. See also Samuel Baker, *The Rise and Progress of London*, London, Ont.: Hayden Press, n.d., p. 17 for confirmation that 'London East is the district of the working men'.
34. *FP*, 16 June, 20 June, 28 June 1916.
35. *FP*, 28 June 1916.
36. *LA*, 28 June 1916.
37. *LA*, 29 August 1918.
38. *FP*, 8 September, 27 September 1919.
39. Beal, 2 December 1918, unpublished report.
40. *ARL* (1912), pp. 34–5.
41. Beal, 22 January, 2 December 1918, unpublished report. See also *ARL* (1912), pp. 24–38.
42. Hogan (1985), op. cit., pp. 175–81.
43. Stamp (1970), op. cit., pp. 422–3.
44. For example, see *FP*, 10 May 1919.
45. Armstrong (1986), op. cit., p. 165. Somerville's sympathies lay primarily with postsecondary education. On 14 January 1914, for example, he had been elected president of the University of Western Ontario and had donated $100,000 to the university for building and equipment costs.
46. *FP*, 29 September 1919.
47. London (1919) *Minutes*, pp. 162–3.
48. *FP*, 4 February 1920.
49. *FP*, 27 April, 28 April, 29 April, 30 April 1920.
50. *FP*, 10 May 1920.

51. *FP*, 4 May 1920.
52. *FP*, 1 June 1921.
53. *FP*, 2 June 1920.
54. *FP*, 2 May 1922.
55. *FP*, 13 May 1922.
56. *FP*, 4 January 1924.
57. *FP*, 29 December 1923.
58. *FP*, 2 January 1924.
59. *FP*, 9 January 1924.
60. *FP*, 12 January 1924.
61. *FP*, 12 January 1924. See also Beal, 12 January 1924, unpublished report.
62. *FP*, 29 January 1924.
63. *FP*, 29 January 1924.
64. *FP*, 29 January 1924.
65. *FP*, 1 February 1924.
66. *FP*, 5 February 1924.
67. London (1924) *Minutes*, p. 26. See also *FP*, 6 February 1924.
68. *FP*, 7 February 1924.
69. London (1924) *Minutes*, pp. 41–3; *FP*, 6 February, 7 February 1924.
70. *FP*, 8 February 1924.
71. *ARL* (1935), p. 84, (1936), p. 69. For Beal's description of the London vocational guidance programme, see his 'Vocational and industrial classes', Ontario Educational Association (1924) *Proceedings*, pp. 290–6. Beal contended that, as early as 1924, 37 per cent of all high school entrance students in the city were attending the Technical School. These figures contrast with Marvin Lazerson and Timothy Dunn's statement that 'vocationalism remained a minor feature of Canadian education' before the Second World War. Lazerson and Dunn (1977), op. cit., p. 288.
72. These data are taken from our examination of student records at the London Technical School beginning 1927.
73. According to Margaret Archer (1979), op. cit., pp. 53–214, this is what European elites have tended to do when confronted with demands for mass schooling. See also Rubinson, R. (1986) Class formation, politics, and institutions: schooling in the United States, *American Journal of Sociology*, 92: 519–48, 526. For the most systematic analysis of the link between schools and the reproduction of the social structure through the distribution of 'cultural capital', see Bourdieu, P. and Passeron, J. C. (1977) *Reproduction in Education, Society, and Culture*, London: Sage Publications.
74. Young. An approach to the study of curricula as socially organized knowledge. In Young, M. F. D. (1971) *Knowledge and Control: New Directions for the Sociology of Education*, London: Collier Macmillan.
75. Kaestle, C. F. (1976) 'Between the scylla of brutal ignorance and the charybdis of a literary education': elite attitudes toward mass schooling in early industrial England and America. In L. Stone (ed.) *Schooling and Society: Studies in the History of Education*, Baltimore: Johns Hopkins University Press: pp. 177–91. See also Kaestle, C. F. (1983) *Pillars of the Republic: Common Schools and American Society, 1780–1860*, New York: Hill and Wang: pp. 33–6.
76. Mason, W. (1921) Who's to weed the onions when everybody is highly educated? *Literary Digest*, 68: 50–52.
77. Archer (1979), op. cit., pp. 53–214.
78. Stamp, R. M. (1978) Canadian high schools in the 1920s and 1930s: the social challenge to the academic tradition, *Canadian Historical Association Papers*, p. 92.

Chapter 6 Subject Status and Curriculum Change: Local Commercial Education, 1920–1940

1. Ontario Legislative Assembly (1902) *Report of the Minister of Education, Province of Ontario, for the Year 1901*, Toronto: p. iv; Ontario Legislative Assembly (1942) *Report of the Minister of Education, Province of Ontario, for the Year 1940*, Toronto: p. 111.
2. The 'post-revisionist' approach challenges both the traditional, celebratory understanding of this period and the later revisionist interpretation. The former school is represented by Cremin, L. A. (1961) *The Transformation of the School*, New York: Knopf. The revisionist approach is best seen in Katz, M. (1968) *The Irony of Early School Reform*, Cambridge, MA: Harvard University Press; Bowles, S. and Gintis, H. (1976) *Schooling in Capitalist America*, New York: Basic; and Lazerson, M. and Dunn, T. (1977) Schools and the work crisis: vocationalism in Canadian education. In H. A. Stevenson and J. D. Wilson (eds) *Precepts, Policy and Process: Perspectives on Contemporary Canadian Education*, London: Alexander, Blake.
3. Kliebard, H. M. (1986) *The Struggle for the American Curriculum, 1893–1958*, London: Routledge; Kantor, H. A. (1988) *Learning to Earn: School, Work and Vocational Reform in California, 1880–1930*, Madison: University of Wisconsin Press; Labaree, D. F. (1988) *The Making of an American High School*, New Haven, CT: Yale University Press. See also Weiss, J. (1982) The advent of education for clerical work in the high school: a reconsideration of the historiography of vocationalism, *Teachers College Record*, 83: 613–38; and Powers, J. B. (1992) *The 'Girl Question' in Education: Vocational Education for Young Women in the Progressive Era*, London, New York and Philadelphia: Falmer Press. For comparison, Harold Silver's British work is of great utility in discerning patterns of vocational education: see Silver, H. (1983) *Education as History: Interpreting Nineteenth and Twentieth Century Education*, London: Methuen.
4. This point is supported by Jane Gaskell's convincing contemporary analysis of the perceptions of female students in commercial courses. See Gaskell, J. (1987) Course enrolment in the high school: the perspective of working-class females. In J. Gaskell and A. McLaren (eds) *Women and Education: a Canadian Perspective*, Calgary: Detselig.
5. Jackson, N. S. and Gaskell, J. S. (1987) White collar vocationalism: the rise of commercial education in Ontario and British Columbia, 1870–1920, *Curriculum Inquiry*, 17: 177–202.
6. Bourdieu, P. and Passeron, J. C. (1977) *Reproduction in Education, Society and Culture*, London: Sage; Deever, B. (1990) Curriculum change and the process of hegemony in an Appalachian community, Paper presented at the Annual Meeting of the American Educational Research Association, Boston; Labaree (1988), op. cit., pp. 33–4.
7. The social construction of subject status has been studied in some depth by historians. See Goodson, I. (1988) *The Making of Curriculum*, London, New York and Philadelphia: Falmer Press.
8. Bourdieu and Passeron (1977), op. cit.; Labaree, D. F. (1986) Curriculum, credentials, and the middle class: a case study of a nineteenth-century high school, *Sociology of Education*, 59: 42–57; and (1988), op. cit.; Deever (1990), op. cit., pp. 3–5; Giroux, H. A. and Penna, A. (1983) Social education in the classroom: the dynamics of the hidden curriculum. In H. Giroux and D. Purpel (eds) *The Hidden Curriculum and Moral Education*, Berkeley, CA: McCutchan; Ringer, F. (1987) Introduction. In D. K. Muller, F. Ringer and B. Simon (eds) *The Rise of the Modern Educational System*, Cambridge: Cambridge University Press.

9. From the 1870s, the Ontario school system included two types of secondary schools: high schools and collegiate institutes. Both taught the normal academic curriculum, with high schools teaching modern languages to males and females, and collegiate institutes teaching the classical languages, mainly to young men. By the twentieth century, this distinction no longer existed. High schools and collegiate institutes enrolled students of both genders, whom they taught an academic curriculum on a college preparatory model, though most graduates went into the workforce, not to higher education. See Gidney, R. D. and Millar, W. P. J. (1990) *Inventing Secondary Education: the Rise of the High School in Nineteenth-century Ontario*, Montreal: McGill-Queen's University Press.

10. London, Board of Education, Advisory Vocational Committee (hereafter AVC) (1922) *Minutes*, p. 4. The AVC was also known as the 'Industrial Advisory Committee' at one point, but for consistency this title will not be used in this work.

11. AVC (1924) *Minutes*, p. 3. Beal's comments reveal his concern with slotting students into specific occupations – a major goal of the social efficiency movement. On Beal's own commitment to social efficiency, see Goodson, I. F. and Dowbiggin, I. R. (1991) Vocational education and school reform: the case of the London (Canada) Technical School, 1900–1930, *History of Education Review*, 20: 39–56.

12. London, Board of Education (1924) *Annual Report*, p. 77; AVC (1925) *Minutes*, p. 3; London Technical and Commercial High School (hereafter LTCHS), Student Record Cards, H.B. Beal Secondary School Archives; interview with Margaret Fallona, 1990. Fallona was a student at the school in the 1920s, and a teacher in the commercial department in the 1930s.

13. London, Board of Education (1926–1933) *Annual Reports*.

14. AVC (1927) *Minutes*, p. 7; (1928), p. 3. Similar courses were introduced elsewhere in North America. See Kantor (1988), op. cit., p. 63, for evidence from California.

15. London, Board of Education (1920–1930) *Minutes*; AVC (1920–1930) *Minutes*.

16. LTCHS, student record cards. See also Jackson and Gaskell (1987), op. cit., p. 192.

17. See Goodson, I. F. and Dowbiggin, I. R. (1989) Gender, class, and vocational schooling: technical education for women in London (Canada), 1870–1935. Beal Project working paper. Of course, even in the home of coeducation itself – the USA – a similar pattern held true. See Rury, J. L. (1984) Vocationalism for home and work: women's education in the United States, 1880–1930, *History of Education Quarterly*, 24: 36–8; Tyack, D. and Hansot, E. (1990) *Learning Together: a History of Coeducation in American Public Schools*, New Haven, CT: Yale University Press; and Powers (1992), op. cit.

18. LTCHS, student record cards; London, Board of Education for the City of London (1921) *Annual Report of the Board of Education for the City of London*, London: Board of Education, pp. 86–8.

19. Jackson and Gaskell (1987), op. cit., pp. 186–7. On commercial education in the United States, see Weiss (1982), op. cit.; Rury (1984), op. cit., pp. 29–34; and Powers (1992), op. cit., Chapters 4 and 10.

20. Dickinson, J. A. (1935) Commercial education in the London schools, *The Tecalogue*, 7–8; AVC (1898–99) *Minutes*, pp. 25–6, 38, 87.

21. London, Board of Education (1899–1900) *Minutes*, pp. 2–3.

22. Gidney and Millar (1990), op. cit., p. 294; Jackson and Gaskell (1987), op. cit., pp. 182–3.

23. For a parallel account describing how the separate physical location of a department allowed for a separate status, see Labaree (1988), op. cit., p. 164.

24. Cited in Jackson and Gaskell (1987), op. cit., p. 193.

25. Ontario, Minister of Education (1914) *Annual Report of the Minister of Education*, Toronto: Legislative Assembly, pp. 84–6; (1922), pp. 260–3.
26. London, Board of Education (1902–3) *Minutes*, pp. 44, 52; (1907), p. 196.
27. London, Board of Education (1908) *Minutes*, pp. 315–16, 355.
28. London, Board of Education (1915) *Minutes*, pp. 53, 130–1.
29. London, Board of Education (1918) *Minutes*, p. 140.
30. London, Board of Education (1919) *Minutes*, p. 53.
31. London, Board of Education (1919) *Minutes*, pp. 84–5, 134–5, 138, 141, 183.
32. Goodson and Dowbiggin (1991), op. cit., pp. 43–4. The best analyses of social efficiency and its effects on education can be found in Kliebard (1986), op. cit., pp. 89–122, and in Franklin, B. M. (1986) *Building the American Community: the School Curriculum and the Search for Social Control*, London, New York and Philadelphia: Falmer, pp. 83–118.
33. AVC (1918) *Minutes*, 22 January. See also London, Board of Education (1912) *Annual Report*, pp. 24–38. The problem was unavoidable though, since the original justification for vocational schooling emphasized its role in making education interesting to those who were not interested in, or suited to, academic work. On this point, see Kantor (1988), op. cit., p. 115.
34. Goodson and Dowbiggin (1991), op. cit., pp. 47–56.
35. *London Free Press* (hereafter *LFP*), 29 December 1923, 2–9 January 1924, 5 February 1924.
36. *LFP*, 29 January to 8 February 1924; London, Board of Education (1924) *Minutes*, pp. 26, 41–3.
37. London, Board of Education (1926) *Minutes*, pp. 350–2.
38. Fallona interview; see also Mann, R. I. (n.d.) Quo Vadis Domini?, clipping found in H.B. Beal Secondary School archives. Gary McCulloch has drawn my attention to a similar expression of opinion in a local rhyme from Christchurch, New Zealand: 'with hob-nailed boots and unwashed neck, they don't come here, they go to Tech.'
39. London, Board of Education (1920–1) *Minutes*; Dickinson (1935), op. cit., p. 8.
40. This happened throughout the province, though other places did not have the excuse of a spectacular fire. See Jackson and Gaskell (1987), op. cit., p. 194.
41. Weiss, J. H. (1978) Educating for clerical work: a history of commercial education in the United States since 1850, EdD thesis, Harvard, pp. 176–7.
42. Doyle, B. (1989) *English and Englishness*, London: Routledge, p. 71.
43. There is some evidence that local educators had tried to increase male attendance through earlier advertising campaigns. Documents from the period 1914 to 1917 contain a series of references to programmes of publicity for commercial education, on the part of the principal of the CI and the Commercial Advisory Committee, and with the approval of the Board of Education. Yet during the same period, the same men (and they were all men) complained that the facilities for commercial classes had become strained to the limit. Why did such an oversubscribed course generate campaigns of recruitment, when other courses did not? A logical answer (though one unsupported by surviving direct evidence) is that the campaign aimed at male, rather than at seeking to increase the absolute numbers of commercial students. See, for example, London, Board of Education (1914) *Minutes*, p. 140; (1915) p. 53; (1916) p. 146; (1917) p. 115; (1918) p. 140.
44. Lowe, G. S. (1986) Women, work and the office: the feminization of clerical occupations in Canada, 1901–1931. In V. Strong-Boag and A. C. Fellman (eds) *Rethinking Canada: the Promise of Women's History*, Toronto: Copp Clark Pitman;

Jackson and Gaskell (1987), op. cit., pp. 184–5; Kantor (1988), op. cit., p. 62; Labaree (1988), op. cit., pp. 166–8.

45. Canada (1931) *Census of Canada*, Ottawa: King's Printer, p. 74.

46. On the philosophy behind domestic science, the alternate vocational option for young women, see Pedersen, D. (1981) 'The scientific training of mothers': the campaign for domestic science in Ontario Schools, 1890–1913. In R. A. Jarrell and A. E. Roos (eds) *Critical Issues in the History of Canadian Science, Technology and Medicine*, Thornhill: HSTC Publications, pp. 178–94; Danylewycz, M., Fahmy-Eid, N. and Thivierge, N. (1984) L'enseignement menager et les 'home economics' au Québec et en Ontario au debut du 20e siecle: une analyse comparee. In J. D. Wilson (ed.) *An Imperfect Past: Education and Society in Canadian History*, Vancouver: University of British Columbia, pp. 106–12; Stamp, R. M. (1977) Teaching girls their 'God given place in life', *Atlantis*, 2(2): 18–34; Dunn, T. A. (1980) Vocationalism and its promoters in British Columbia 1900–1929, *The Journal of Educational Thought*, 14: 91–107; Crowley, T. (1986) Madonnas before Magdalenes: Adelaide hoodless and the making of the Canadian Gibson girl, *Canadian Historical Review*, 67: 520–1. The Canadian movement was informed and inspired by similar campaigns in Britain and the United States. On these, see: Purvis, J. (1985) Domestic subjects since 1870. In Goodson, I. F. (ed.) *Social Histories of the Secondary Curriculum*, London and Philadelphia: Falmer Press; Yoxall, A. (1913) *A History of the Teaching of Domestic Economy*. Reprinted Bath: Chivers, 1965; and Rury (1984), op. cit., pp. 21–44.

47. Posen, G. (1980) The office boom: the relationship between the expansion of the female clerical labour force and the response of the public education system, 1900–1940, Toronto: Ontario Institute for Studies in Education, photocopy. We wish to thank Jane Gaskell for supplying us with a copy of this paper. See also Ontario, Minister of Education (1920) *Annual Report*, p. 250; (1925) p. 216; (1930) p. 352.

48. Ontario, Minister of Education (1930) *Annual Report*, p. 352; Weiss (1982), op. cit., p. 627; Rury (1984), op. cit., pp. 30–3; Powers (1992), op. cit., pp. 113–27.

49. Canada (1911) *Census of Canada*, v. 6, p. 340; (1921) v. 4, pp. 432–4; (1941) v. 7, p. 238.

50. London, Board of Education (1902–3) *Minutes*, pp. 5–9, 52.

51. London, Board of Education (1921) *Annual Report*, p. 89; LTCHS, student record cards. For data from 1927 and 1929, see Goodson and Dowbiggin (1989), op. cit., pp. 32–3.

52. Ontario, Minister of Education (1930) *Annual Report*, p. 353; London, Board of Education (1940) *Annual Report*, pp. 72–3. This feminization of commercial studies clearly took place at the expense of domestic technical subjects. In 1923 almost twice as many first year female students chose commercial studies as chose the general domestic curriculum. In later years the discrepancy grew; almost five hundred young women enrolled in commercial classes in 1930 contrasted sharply with only 147 registered in domestic technical courses. In 1940, the 70 female winners of commercial certificates far outnumbered the 21 female students who took certificates in home economics. LTCHS, Student Record Cards; Ontario, Minister of Education (1930) *Annual Report*, pp. 352–3; London, Board of Education (1940) *Annual Report*, pp. 72–3. These statistics differ markedly from the rough estimates presented by Danylewycz *et al.* (1984), op. cit., p. 103, who claimed that twice as many young women took domestic subjects as commercial studies in technical schools at this time.

53. London, Board of Education (1898–1940) *Annual Reports*.

54. London, Board of Education (1920) *Minutes*, p. 93.
55. London, Board of Education (1931) *Minutes*, appendix, n.p.
56. See London, Board of Education (1923) *Minutes*, pp. 43–51; (1928) pp. 30–4.
57. London, Board of Education (1915) *Minutes*, p. 143; Fallona interview.
58. Fallona interview; see also London, Board of Education (1921) *Minutes*, p. 201.
59. London, Board of Education (1933) *Minutes*, p. 58; Fallona interview.
60. London, Board of Education (1905) *Minutes*, p. 95.
61. Fallona interview.
62. Jackson and Gaskell (1987), op. cit., pp. 193–4; also see Kantor (1988), op. cit., pp. 123–48.
63. Table 3 was constructed from the Minister of Education's *Report* as follows: 'Non-manual' represents the sum of the *Report* categories titled 'Commerce,' 'Law, medicine, dentistry and the Church' and 'Teaching'. 'Skilled manual' is identical to the category title 'The trades', while 'Manual unskilled' is the same as the category 'Labouring occupations'. The categories titled 'Agriculture', 'Other occupation' and 'No occupation' from the *Report* were ignored in the construction of the table.
64. LTCHS, student record cards; Fallona interview; interview with Pearl Morgan, 10 June 1989. Morgan taught in the technical school at the time.
65. Morgan interview.
66. See, for example, Lazerson and Dunn (1977), op. cit.; Dunn, op. cit.; Morrison, T. R. (1974) Reform as social tracking: the case of industrial education in Ontario 1870–1900, *Journal of Educational Thought*, 8(2): 88–110. For similar American interpretations, consult: Lazerson, M. and Grubb, W. (1974) *American Education and Vocationalism: A Documentary History, 1870–1970*, New York: Teachers College Press; Kantor, H. A. and Tyack, D. (eds) (1982) *Work, Youth and Schooling*, Stanford, CA: Stanford University Press; Labaree (1988), op. cit.; Kantor (1988), op. cit.; and Powers (1992), op. cit.

Chapter 7   'Nations at Risk' and 'National Curriculum': Ideology and Identity

1. I have employed the term 'United Kingdom' as a statement of a particular governmental aspiration towards national identity. In many ways it links with a broader project of privileging a particular form of 'Englishness' (a form with which I personally have no empathy or sympathy). In the event, as the National Curriculum proceeds it is leading to a fragmented response in the different 'kingdoms' – Scotland, for instance, has managed to modify the testing requirements for the 'National' Curriculum.
2. Subjects here might be read in both senses, as we shall see: the institutionalized school subject and the subjectivities that those institutionalized subjects seek to implant and patrol.
3. This section was written before the withdrawal of the UK pound from the European Exchange Rate Mechanism and the effective devaluation of the pound, and of course before the replacement of Thatcher by Major.
4. Fowler, W. S. (1988) *Towards the National Curriculum*, London: Kogan Page, p. 38.
5. Quoted, ibid., pp. 59–60.
6. Subsequently these bodies were merged.
7. Department of Education and Science (1989) *National Curriculum History Group Interim Report*, quoted *Times Educational Supplement*, 18 August: 4.

8. Ibid., *Times Educational Supplement.*
9. Ibid.
10. Ibid.
11. Ryder, J. and Silver, H. (1970) *Modern English Society, History and Structure 1850–1970*, London: Methuen.
12. Eaglesham, E. J. R. (1967) *The Foundations of Twentieth-century Education in England*, London: Routledge & Kegan Paul, p. 59.
13. Ibid., pp. 59–60.
14. Rubinstein, D. and Simon, B. (1973) *The Evolution of the Comprehensive School 1926–1972*, London: Routledge & Kegan Paul, p. 123.
15. Kerr, J. (1971) The problem of curriculum reform. In R. Hooper (ed.) *The Curriculum Context, Design and Development*, Edinburgh: Oliver & Boyd, pp. 178–200.
16. Department of Education and Science (1989), op. cit.
17. Moon, B. and Mortimore, P. (1989) *The National Curriculum: Straitjacket or Safety Net?* London: Colophon Press, p. 9.
18. *The Times*, 22 October 1989.
19. Holmes, E. G. A. (1928) *What Is and What Might Be*. London: Constable, p. 103.
20. Ibid., pp. 103–5.
21. Ibid., pp. 106–8.
22. Reference quoted in Chitty, C. (1988) Central control of the school curriculum, 1944–87, *History of Education*, 17(4): 321–34.
23. Broder, D. S. (1989) Mrs Thatcher and the erosion of British liberty, *Guardian Weekly*, 141(5): 7.
24. Corrigan, P. (1990) *Social Forms/Human Capacities*, London and New York: Routledge.
25. See Goodson, I. F. (1988) and (1993). North American readers unfamiliar with the shorthand way in which I have dealt with issues of social structure may need to refer to these books to examine the argument in greater detail.

Chapter 8   Studying Curriculum: Social Constructionist Perspectives

1. Parts of this chapter were written as the invited Keynote Address to the Fifth International Congress of the Nordic Educational Research Association held at the University of Uppsala in March 1989 and published in 1990 in the *Journal of Curriculum Studies*, 22(4): 299–312.
2. Reid, W. A. (1978) *Thinking About the Curriculum*, London: Routledge & Kegan Paul, p. 17.
3. Goodson, I. F. (1993) *School Subjects and Curriculum Change*, 3rd edn, London, New York and Philadelphia: Falmer Press.
4. Goodson, I. F. (ed.) (1985) *Social Histories of the Secondary Curriculum*, London and Philadelphia: Falmer Press.
5. McCulloch, G., Jenkins, E. and Layton, D. (1985) *Technological Revolution?* London and Philadelphia: Falmer Press.
6. McCulloch, G. (1989) *The Secondary Technical School*, London, New York and Philadelphia: Falmer Press.
7. Woolnough, B. E. (1988) *Physics Teaching in Schools 1960–85: of People, Policy and Power*, London, New York and Philadelphia: Falmer Press.
8. Cooper, B. (1985) *Renegotiating Secondary School Mathematics*, London and Philadelphia: Falmer Press.

9. Moon, B. (1986) *The 'New Maths' Curriculum Controversy*, London, New York and Philadelphia: Falmer Press.

10. Kliebard, H. (1986) *The Struggle for the American Curriculum 1893–1953*, London: Routledge and Kegan Paul.

11. Franklin, B. (1986) *Building the American Community*, London, New York and Philadelphia: Falmer Press.

12. Popkewitz, T. S. (ed.) (1987) *The Formation of School Subjects: the Struggle for Creating an American Institution*, London, New York and Philadelphia: Falmer Press.

13. Tomkins, G. S. (1986) *A Common Countenance: Stability and Change in the Canadian Curriculum*, Scarborough, Prentice-Hall.

14. Rowell, P. M. and Gaskell, P. J. (1988) Tensions and realignments: school physics in British Columbia 1955–80. In I. F. Goodson (ed.) *International Perspectives in Curriculum History*, London and New York: Routledge.

15. Goodson, I. F. (ed.) (1988) *International Perspectives in Curriculum History*, 2nd edn, London and New York: Routledge.

16. Cunningham, P. (1988) *Curriculum Change in the Primary School since 1945*, London, New York and Philadelphia: Falmer Press.

17. Musgrave, P. W. (1988) *Whose Knowledge?* London, New York and Philadelphia: Falmer Press.

18. Powers, J. B. (1992) *The Girl Question in Education: Vocational Education for Young Women in the Progressive Era*, London, New York and Philadelphia: Falmer Press.

19. Meyer, J. W., Kamens, D. H., Benavot, A. with Cha, Y. K. and Wong, S. Y. (1992) *School Knowledge for the Masses*, London, New York and Philadelphia: Falmer Press.

20. Goodson, I. F. (1990) Laronplansforskning: mot ett socialt konstruktivistiskt perspektiv, *Forskning om utbildning*, 1: 4–18; Goodson, I. F. (1990) A social history of subjects, *Scandinavian Journal of Educational Research*, 34(2): 111–21; Goodson, I. F. (1990) Zur Sozialgeschichte der Schulfacher, *Bildung und Erziehung*, December: 379–89; Goodson, I. F. (1991) La construccion del curriculum: posibilidades y ambitos de investigacion de la historia del curriculum, *Revista de Educacion*, 295: 7–37; Goodson, I. F. (1991) Tornando-se una materia academica: padroes de explicacao e evolucao, *Teoria and Educacao* (Brazil), 2: 230–54; Goodson, I. F. and Dowbiggin, I. R. (1991) Vocational education and school reform: the case of the London (Canada) Technical School, 1990–1930, *History of Education Review*, 20(1): 39–60.

21. Watson, F. (1909) *The Beginning of the Teaching of Modern Subjects in England*, London: Pitman.

22. Goodson, I. F. (in the press) Basil Bernstein and aspects of the sociology of the curriculum. In P. Atkinson, S. Delamont and B. Davies (eds) *Reproduction and Discourse*, Cresskill, NJ: Hampton Press.

23. Goodson, I. F. (1988) *The Making of Curriculum: Collected Essays*, London, New York and Philadelphia: Falmer Press; Goodson, I. F. (forthcoming) *Studying School Subjects*, London, New York and Philadelphia: Falmer Press; Goodson, I. F. (forthcoming) *The Changing Curriculum*, New York: Peter Lang.

24. Goodson, I. F. and Walker, R. (1991) *Biography, Identity and Schooling*, London, New York and Philadelphia: Falmer Press; Goodson, I. F. (ed.) (1992) *Studying Teachers' Lives*, New York: Teachers College Press; Goodson, I. F. (forthcoming) *Representing Teachers*, New York: Teachers College Press; London: Cassell.

25. Goodson (1988), op. cit., p. 112.

26. Goodson (1993), op. cit., pp. 3–4.

27. Hobsbawm, E. (1985) Introduction: inventing traditions. In E. Hobsbawm and T. Ranger (eds) *The Invention of Tradition*, Cambridge: Cambridge University Press, p. 1.

28. Shipman, M. D., Bolam, D. and Jenkins, D. R. (1974) *Inside a Curriculum Project: a Case Study in the Process of Curriculum Change*, London: Methuen, p. 2.

Recent Publications by the Author

(1983) *School Subjects and Curriculum Change*, London, Sydney and Dover, NH: Croom Helm.

(1983) Subjects for study: aspects of a social history of curriculum, *Journal of Curriculum Studies*, Autumn, 15(4): 391–408.

(1983) Defining and defending the subject. In A. Hargreaves and M. Hammersley (eds) *Sociology of Curriculum Practice*, London and Philadelphia: Falmer Press.

(1983) Life histories and teaching. In M. Hammersley (ed.) *The Ethnography of Schooling*, Driffield: Nafferton.

With S. J. Ball (eds) (1984) *Defining the Curriculum: Histories and Ethnographies*, London and Philadelphia: Falmer Press.

With H. Oonk and C. Scurati (1984) *Curriculum Models on European Education*, Alkmaar, Netherlands: CEVNO.

With S. J. Ball (1984) Introduction: defining the curriculum; histories and ethnographies. In I. F. Goodson and S. J. Ball (eds) *Defining the Curriculum: Histories and Ethnographies*, London and Philadelphia: Falmer Press, pp. 1–12.

(1984) Subjects for study: towards a social history of curriculum. In I. F. Goodson and S. J. Ball (eds) *Defining the Curriculum: Histories and Ethnographies*, London and Philadelphia: Falmer Press, pp. 25–44.

(1984) Beyond the subject monolith. In P. Harling (ed.) *New Directions in Educational Leadership*, London and Philadelphia: Falmer Press.

(1984) Defining a subject for the comprehensive school: a case study. In S. Ball (ed.) *Comprehensive Schooling: a Reader*, London, and Philadelphia: Falmer Press.

With S. J. Ball (eds) (1985) *Teachers' Lives and Careers*, London, New York and Philadelphia: Falmer Press.

(1985, ed.) *Social Histories of the Secondary Curriculum: Subjects for Study*, London, New York and Philadelphia: Falmer Press.

With V. McGivney (1985) *European Dimensions in the Secondary School Curriculum*, London, New York and Philadelphia: Falmer Press.

(1985) Towards curriculum history. In I. F. Goodson (ed.) *Social Histories of the Secondary Curriculum: Subjects for Study*, London and Philadelphia: Falmer Press, pp. 1–8.

(1985) Subjects for study: case studies in curriculum history. In I. F. Goodson (ed.) *Social Histories of the Secondary Curriculum: Subjects for Study*, London and Philadelphia: Falmer Press, pp. 9–17.

(1985) Subjects for study. In I. F. Goodson (ed.) *Social Histories of the Secondary Curriculum: Subjects for Study*, London and Philadelphia: Falmer Press, pp. 343–67.

(1985) History context and qualitative method. In R. C. Burgess (ed.) *Strategies for Educational Research*, London, New York and Philadelphia: Falmer Press, pp. 121–51.

(1986) Geoff Whitty's Sociology and School Knowledge: a review, *Journal of Education Policy*, 1(2): 204–5.

(1987) *School Subjects and Curriculum Change*, rev. edn, London, New York and Philadelphia: Falmer Press.

(1987) (ed.) *International Perspectives in Curriculum History*, London, Sydney and Dover, NH: Croom Helm.

(1987) Introduction. In I. F. Goodson (ed.) *International Perspectives in Curriculum History*, London, Sydney and Dover, NH: Croom Helm.

(1987) On understanding curriculum: the alienation of curriculum theory, *Curriculum Perspectives*, 7(2): 41–7.

(1987) Tomkins' *Common Countenance*: a Review, *History of Education*, 17(3): 249–51.

(1988) *The Making of Curriculum: Collected Essays*, London, New York and Philadelphia: Falmer Press.

(1988, ed.) *International Perspectives in Curriculum History*, London and New York: Routledge.

(1988) Three curricular traditions and their implications. In R. Dale, R. Fergusson and A. Robinson (eds) *Frameworks for Teaching*, London: Hodder and Stoughton, pp. 217–19.

(1988) Beyond the subject monolith. In A. Westoby (ed.) *Culture and Power in Educational Organizations*, Milton Keynes and Philadelphia: Open University Press, pp. 181–97.

(1988) Putting life into educational research. In R. Webb and R. Sherman (eds) *Qualitative Studies in Education*, London, New York and Philadelphia: Falmer Press, pp. 110–22.

With S. J. Ball (eds) (1989) *Teachers' Lives and Careers*, London, New York and Philadelphia: Falmer Press (Open University Set Book Edition).

With G. Milburn and R. J. Clark (eds) (1989) *Reinterpreting Curriculum Research: Images and Arguments*, London, New York and Philadelphia: Falmer Press; London, Ontario: Althouse Press.

With S. J. Ball (1989) Understanding teachers: concepts and contexts. In S. J. Ball and I. F. Goodson (eds) *Teachers' Lives and Careers*, London, New York and Philadelphia: Falmer.

With I. Dowbiggin (1989) Docile bodies: commonalities in the history of psychiatry and schooling, *Qualitative Studies in Education*, 2(3): 203–20.

(1989) Curriculum reform and curriculum theory: a case of historical amnesia, *Cambridge Journal of Education*, July, 131–41.

(1989) Understanding/undermining hierarchy and hegemony. Critical introduction to A. Hargreaves, *Curriculum and Assessment Reform*, Milton Keynes and Philadelphia: Open University Press, pp. 1–14.

With J. M. Mangan and V. A. Rhea (eds) (1989) *Research Strategy for Computers in Education*, interim report 1 from the project Curriculum and Context in the Use of Computers for Classroom Learning. London, Ontario: Faculty of Education, University of Western Ontario.

With J. M. Mangan and V. A. Rhea (eds) (1989) *Emergent Themes in Classroom Computing*, interim report 2 from the project Curriculum and Context in the Use of Computers for Classroom Learning. London, Ontario: Faculty of Education, University of Western Ontario.

With P. Medway (eds) (1990) *Bringing English to Order*, London, New York and Philadelphia: Falmer Press.

With P. Medway (1990) Introduction. In I. F. Goodson and P. Medway (eds) *Bringing English to Order*, London, New York and Philadelphia: Falmer Press, pp. vii–xv.

(1990) Zur Sozialgeschichte der Schulfacher, *Bildung und Erziehung*, December: 379–89.

(1990) Nations at risk, *Journal of Education Policy, Politics of Education Association Yearbook*, 219–32.

(1990) Studying curriculum: towards a social constructionist prospective, *Journal of Curriculum Studies*, 22(4): 299–312.

(1990) Subjects for study: research agenda, *Journal of Curriculum and Supervision*, 5(3): 260–8.

(1990) Laronplansforskning: mot ett socialt konstruktivistiskt perspektiv. *Forskning om utbildning*, 1: 4–18.

(1990) Curriculum history: knowledge and professionalization, *Curriculum and Teaching*, 5(1/2): 3–13.

(1990) A social history of subjects, *Scandinavian Journal of Educational Research*, 34(2): 111–21.

(1990) Social history of school subjects. Section in *International Encyclopedia of Education*, Supplementary Volume 2, Oxford: Pergamon Press, pp. 543–7.

(1990) National Curriculum: ideology and identity. In *Studies in Education*, London, New York and Philadelphia: Falmer Press, chapter 7.

(1990) Why study school subjects? In H. Haft and S. Hopmann (eds) *Case Studies in Curriculum Administration History*, London, New York and Philadelphia: Falmer.

With I. Dowbiggin (1990) Commonalities in the history of school subjects in psychiatry. In S. J. Ball (ed.) *Foucault and Education*, London: Routledge and Kegan Paul, pp. 105–92.

(1990) Teachers' lives. In J. Allen and J. Goetz (eds) *Qualitative Research in Education*, Athens, Georgia: University of Georgia, pp. 150–60.

With C. Fliesser and A. Cole (1990) Induction of community college instructors. From the Interim Report of the project Studying Teacher Development. London, Ontario: Faculty of Education, University of Western Ontario, pp. 50–6.

With J. M. Mangan and V. A. Rhea (eds) (1990) *Illuminative Evaluation of Classroom Computing*, interim report 3 from the project Curriculum and Context in the Use of Computers for Classroom Learning. London, Ontario: Faculty of Education, University of Western Ontario.

With J. M. Mangan and V. A. Rhea (eds) (1990) *Teacher Development and Computer Use in Schools*, interim report 4 from the project Curriculum and Context in the Use of Computers for Classroom Learning. London, Ontario: Faculty of Education, University of Western Ontario.

With R. Walker (1991) *Biography, Identity and Schooling*, London, New York and Philadelphia: Falmer Press.

With I. Dowbiggin (1991) Vocational education and school reform, *History of Education Review*, 20(1): 39–60.

(1991) School subjects: patterns of change, *Curriculum and Teaching*, 3–11.

(1991) La construccion del curriculum: posibilidades y ambitos de investigacion de la historia del curriculum. *Revista de Educacion*, 295: 7–37.

With M. Apple and J. Meyer (eds) (1991) Special Issue of *Sociology of Education* on sociology of curriculum.

(1991) Sponsoring the teacher's voice, *Cambridge Journal of Education*, 21(1): 35–45.

(1991) Tornando-se una materia academica: padroes de explicacao e evolucao. *Teoria and Educacao* (Brazil), 2: 230–54.

(1991) Nations at risk and national curriculum. Section in *Handbook of the American Politics of Education Association*, pp. 219–32.

(1991) Curriculum reform and historical amnesia. In R. Moon (ed.) *New Curriculum – National Curriculum*, London: Hodder and Stoughton.

With J. M. Mangan (ed.) (1991) *Qualitative Studies in Educational Research: Methodologies in Transition*, RUCCUS Occasional Papers Volume 1, University of Western Ontario.

With J. M. Mangan (ed.) (1991) *Computers, Classrooms, and Culture: Studies in the Use of Computers for Classroom Learning*, RUCCUS Occasional Papers Volume 2, University of Western Ontario.

With J. M. Mangan (1991) An alternative paradigm for educational research. From the project Studying Teacher Development. London, Ontario: Faculty of Education, University of Western Ontario.

(1991) Studying teacher's lives: problems and possibilities. From the project Studying Teacher Development. London, Ontario: Faculty of Education, University of Western Ontario.

With J. M. Mangan and V. A. Rhea (eds) (1991) *Curriculum and Context*, Volume 1 of the Summative Report from the project Curriculum and Context in the Use of Computers for Classroom Learning. London, Ontario: Faculty of Education, University of Western Ontario.

With J. M. Mangan and V. A. Rhea (eds) (1991) *The Use of Computers for Classroom Learning*, Volume 2 of the Summative Report from the project Curriculum and Context in the Use of Computers for Classroom Learning. London, Ontario: Faculty of Education, University of Western Ontario.

With J. M. Mangan and V. A. Rhea (eds) (1991) *Closing the Circle: Conclusions and Recommendations*, Volume 3 of the Summative Report from the project Curriculum and Context in the Use of Computers for Classroom Learning. London, Ontario: Faculty of Education, University of Western Ontario.

With J. M. Mangan and V. A. Rhea (eds) (1991) *Classroom Cultures and the Introduction of Computers*, Interim Report 5 from the project Curriculum and Context in the Use of Computers for Classroom Learning. London, Ontario: Faculty of Education, University of Western Ontario.

(1992, ed.) *Studying Teachers' Lives*, London and New York: Routledge.

(1992) Sponsoring the teacher's voice. In M. Fullan and A. Hargreaves (eds) *Understanding Teacher Development*, London: Cassell; New York: Teachers College Press.

With J. M. Mangan (1992) Computers in schools as symbolic and ideological action: the genealogy of the ICON, *The Curriculum Journal*, 3(3): 261–76.

(1992) Studying school subjects, *Curriculum Perspectives*, 12(1): 23–6.

(1992) Studying teachers' lives: an emergent field of inquiry. In I. F. Goodson (ed.) *Studying Teachers' Lives*, London and New York: Routledge, pp. 1–17.

(1992) Studying teachers' lives: problems and possibilities. In I. F. Goodson (ed.) *Studying Teachers' Lives*, London and New York: Routledge, pp. 234–49.

(1992) School subjects: patterns of stability, *Education Research and Perspectives*, 19(1): 52–64.

(1992) On curriculum form, *Sociology of Education*, 65(1): 66–75.

(1992) Dar voz ao professor: as historias de vida dos professores e o seu desenvolvimento profissional. In A. Novoa (ed.) *Vidas De Professores*, Porto: Porto Editora, pp. 63–78.

(1992) 'Nations at risk' and 'national curriculum': ideology and identity. In J. Lynch, C. Modgil and S. Modgil (eds) *Equity or Excellence? Education and Cultural Reproduction*, London, New York and Philadelphia: Falmer Press, pp. 199–213.

With J. M. Mangan (eds) (1992) *History, Context, and Qualitative Methods in the Study of Education*, RUCCUS Occasional Papers Volume 3, University of Western Ontario.

(1993) *School Subjects and Curriculum Change*, 3rd edn, London, New York and Philadelphia: Falmer Press.

With C. J. Anstead (1993) Subject status and curriculum change: commercial education in London, Ontario, 1920–1940, *Paedagogica Historica*, 29(2).

(1993) Studying the teacher's life and work, *Teaching and Teacher Education*.

(1993) Investigating schooling: from the personal to the programmatic, *New Education*, 14(1): 11–20.

With C. J. Anstead (1993) *Through the Schoolhouse Door*, Toronto: Garamond Press.

With C. J. Anstead (1993) On explaining curriculum change, *The Curriculum Journal*, 4(3).

(1993) Forms of knowledge and teacher education, *Journal of Education for Teaching Papers*, 1: 217–29.

Index